AKENSIDE, MACPI

MARK AKENSIDE
JAMES MACPHERSON
EDWARD YOUNG

Selected Poetry

*Edited with an Introduction and Notes
by S.H. Clark*

FyfieldBooks

The author wishes to thank the British Academy for the post-doctoral fellowship during which this selection was prepared.

First published in 1994 by
Carcanet Press Limited
208-212 Corn Exchange Buildings
Manchester M4 3BQ

A CIP catalogue record for this book
is available from the British Library.
ISBN 0 85635 927 0

The publisher acknowledges financial assistance
from the Arts Council of Great Britain

Set in 10pt Palatino by Bryan Williamson, Frome
Printed and bound in England by SRP Ltd, Exeter

Contents

Three Poets of Sensibility

To write an introduction to the poetry of sensibility seems inevitably to mean writing an apology for it. I have grave reservations about using the term at all, and doubt whether it can ever be fully rehabilitated. It evokes something poignant and ineffectual; clouds the differences between highly-gifted and individual figures; and ultimately endorses their status as much-disparaged and little-read. Amid all the turbulent revisionism of twentieth century literary criticism, this movement has been held in continuously low esteem. This can be seen simply in terms of the publishing history of the three authors in this volume. No-one has felt inclined, out of artistic respect, historical interest, or even antiquarian charity, to reprint either Akenside or Young since the mid-nineteenth century. Macpherson falls into a special category because of his claim to be translating the words of Ossian, an ancient Scottish Bard (as late as 1926, W.S. Sharp produced an edition blithely asserting the authenticity of this persona), but there has been little or no dissent from Johnson's verdict: 'as a modern production it is nothing'.[1]

But the alternative term for the poetry produced between, roughly speaking, 1730 and 1780, pre-Romanticism, carries its own restrictive premises. It assumes that these poets are best regarded as part of a continuous evolution towards the later movement, and so relegates them to a perpetual precursordom. This absence of literary autonomy has meant that their writing has all too often been dissolved back into its constituent elements, a legitimate quarry for excavation by the history of ideas. The implicit working premiss has tended to be that it is all done better by Wordsworth. Better, perhaps, but necessarily differently, and it will be helpful to glance briefly at *Tintern Abbey* in order to avoid over-simplifying this relation. The poem is obviously, in the most general sense, the descendant of eighteenth-century meditative blank verse; the solitary meditation over childhood haunts suggests Gray's 'Ode on a Distant Prospect of Eton College'. The regenerating movement inwards from the 'wild and secluded scene' to 'thoughts of more deep seclusion' (6-7) is also a familiar feature of the topographic verse tradition, particularly in its ambivalent straddling of analogy (the order in the landscape parallels the order in the mind, as both are parts of a benevolent creation) and associationism (the poet's mind has been imbued with, or even literally created out of, the sense-data received from his locality). The local texture of Wordsworth's rhetoric can be linked to his immediate predecessors with equal ease. For example, the famous evocation of

> a sense sublime
> Of something far more deeply interfused,
> Whose dwelling is the light of setting suns,
> And the round ocean and the living air,
> And the blue sky, and in the mind of man:
> A motion and a spirit, that impels
> All thinking things, all objects of all thought,
> And rolls through all things.   (95-102)

has multiple analogues in the poetry of sensibility. In Young's *Night Thoughts*, we find

> Look Nature through, 'tis Revolution All;
> All Change, no Death . . . All, to reflourish, fades.
> As in a wheel, All sinks to re-ascend . . .
> The world of matter with its various forms,
> All dies into new Life, Life born from Death
> Rolls the vast Mass, and shall for ever roll.
>   (6:677-8; 687-8; 696-8)

This, I think, brings out well the Newtonian impersonality of Wordsworth's communion with the divine 'presence'. A more Platonic dimension is revealed through comparison with a passage from Akenside's *The Pleasures of Imagination*, where the 'something far more deeply interfused' is precisely identified with an act of divine emanation. At the creation, the 'almighty One' contemplates 'The forms eternal of created things', and decides to summon into existence 'The radiant sun, the moon's nocturnal lamp,/ The mountains, woods, and streams, the rolling globe' (1:66-9):

8

> Hence the breath
> Of life informing each organic frame,
> Hence the green earth, and wild resounding waves;
> Hence life and shade alternate; warmth and cold;
> And clear autumnal skies and vernal showers,
> And all the fair variety of things.   (1:73-8)

There are fainter but still discernible echoes of Macpherson in the all-encompassing 'dwelling-place' of memory (l.141), the abrupt disjunction from a past self – 'I cannot paint/ What then I was' (75-6) – and the tonal colouring of the invocations of nature (particularly the closing apostrophe to Dorothy, 'let the moon/ Shine on thee in thy solitary walk' (134-5)). A more specific link can be drawn between the opening lines of *Tintern Abbey*, that so powerfully foreshadow the 'spirit' that 'rolls through things', and Ossian's characteristic apostrophes to the past, for example in 'Cath-Loda' and 'Oina-Morul'.

> Five years hath past; five summers, with the length
> Of five long winters! and again I hear
> The waters, rolling from their mountain-springs
> With a soft inland murmur. (1-4)

> Whence is the stress of years? Whither do they roll along?
> Where have they hid, in mist, their many-coloured sides?

> It is the voice of years that are gone! They roll before me,
> with all their deeds. I seize the tales, as they pass, and
> pour them forth in song.

What is proved by such juxtapositions? Most obviously, that the composite nature of Wordsworth's poetic voice makes the claim of the *Preface to Lyrical Ballads* to represent a decisive break from the 'gaudy and inane phraseology' of the previous generation look decidedly vulnerable.[2] And as for 'poetic diction', it is Wordsworth, rather than Young and Akenside, who is made to look conceptually diffuse by the comparison; and the extracts from Macpherson are of a limpid, if metrically mannered, simplicity.

9

Even these brief extracts indicate that the poets of sensibility are at least fit to stand comparison with their successors. Why then should they have fallen into such utter critical disrepute? Efforts at historical reconstruction have tended to be conducted in a spirit of faint-hearted mitigation; the problem that they set themselves is not so much how this poetry can now be read, as how anyone could ever have taken it seriously. Yet the charges levelled against the movement can easily be shown to be contradictory. The poetry of sensibility is berated for being simultaneously too cerebral and too emotional; too responsive to the thought currents of its own time, and yet shying away from contemporary social reality; both quiveringly hypersensitive and cynically manipulative. But few critics seem inclined to dispute that the line is blighted, cowed, and marginal.

These objections can be reduced to three separate lines of argument.

1) that where the eighteenth-century novel assimilates, explores, enters into active social engagement, the poetry of sensibility retreats into a pastoral introspection devoid of any narrative or dramatic content.

2) that it failed to come to terms with the rationalist ethos of the Augustans, deliberately abstained from the political and social life of its culture, with a resultant self-destructive excess in both the lives and literature of its exponents.

3) that in its despairing attempts at independence, it turned to models, in particular Milton, which it could not productively transform, and which eventually come to signify little more than an 'involuntary homage' to the style that it transgressed.[3]

I think it must immediately be conceded that this poetry lacks the vigorous social mimesis of the emergent eighteenth-century novel. But so has virtually all poetry written since this time, and criticism might perhaps be better engaged in defining what it might positively offer. And it should also be added that the novelists, with the partial exception of Richardson, prove to be

A Note on the Texts

The text for Akenside is usually based on *The Poems of Mark Akenside M.D.* (London, 1770). This stays relatively close to the 1744 edition of *The Pleasures of Imagination* with slightly less capitalisation and numerous minor syntactical corrections. A case could often be made for preferring the original, more fluid, punctuation, but I have chosen not to conflate editions. In some cases I have chosen to emend the idiosyncratic use of the lower case in this edition, notably for the first person (i). The text for 'Hymn to Science' is taken from *The Gentleman's Magazine* (Nov. 1739); that of the *Epistle to Curio* from the edition published in London 1744.

The text for Macpherson is usually taken from Malcolm Laing's *The Poems of Ossian &c., containing the Poetical Works of James Macpherson Esq. in Prose and Rhyme with Notes and Illustrations*, 2 vols (Edinburgh, 1805), based on *The Poems of Ossian by J. Macpherson*, 2 vols, fourth edition revised (London, 1773). Changes made between the first and later editions by Macpherson are comparatively slight, usually in the direction of further simplification of style and occasional excision of conceits. The text for *Fragments of Ancient Poetry. Collected in the Highlands of Scotland, and translated from the Gallic or Erse Language* is from the first edition (Edinburgh, 1760).

For Young, texts for *The Last Day* from the first edition (London, 1713) and for *Love of Fame* from the revised second edition (London, 1728). I have not followed any single text of *Night Thoughts*, but used first editions of individual nights; 'Some Thoughts occasion'd by the present Juncture', is attached to the ninth night (London, 1745). There is no typographical consistency between the different sections; and a major alteration of idiom occurs between the publication of nights six and seven with Young's move to a different publisher. I have chosen to remove the use of italics and block capitals in the interest of greater accessibility; but usually retained variant spellings and oddities of punctuation.

The procedures of regularisation employed by Victorian editors have done a disservice to their authors: Akenside tends to be transformed into a rather vapid proto-Romantic by selective capitalisation of Nature, Beauty, and similar entities, whereas the original is far brisker, more rigorously argumentative; and any attempt to rehabilitate Young must seek to respect rather than domesticate the anarchic nature of his text with its sudden exfoliations, internal rupturing, and distinctive weightlessness. Consequently my working principle has been to avoid modernisation where possible and to try to give a reasonably close approximation to the eighteenth-century text.

Suggested Reading

MARK AKENSIDE

The Poetical Works of Mark Akenside, ed. Robin Dix (Fairleigh Dickinson UP, 1994)

M.H. Abrams, *The Mirror and the Lamp: Romantic Theory and the Critical Tradition* (OUP, 1953)

Jeffrey Hart, 'Akenside's Revisions to "The Pleasures of Imagination"', *PMLA* 74 (1959), 67-74

Geoffrey Hartman, 'Evening Star and Evening Land' in *The Fate of Reading* (Chicago UP, 1975), 147-78

Samuel Johnson, 'Mark Akenside' in *Lives of the English Poets* ed. G. Birkbeck Hill, 3 vols (Oxford, 1905), 411-20

John Mahoney, 'Addison and Akenside: the Impact of Psychological Criticism on Early English Romantic Poetry', *British Journal of Aesthetics* 6 (1966), 365-74

Robert Marsh, 'Addison and Akenside: the Problem of Ideational Debt', *Modern Philology* 59 (1961-2), 36-48

John Sitter, 'Theodicy at Mid-century: Young, Akenside and Hume', *Eighteenth Century Studies* 12 (1978), 90-106; reprinted in *Literary Loneliness in Mid-Eighteenth Century England* (Cornell UP, 1982)

Earl Wasserman. 'Nature Moralised: the Divine Analogy in the Eighteenth Century', *ELH* 20 (1953), 39-76

— 'The English Romantics: the Grounds of Knowledge', *Studies in Romanticism* 4 (1964), 17-34

JAMES MACPHERSON

James Macpherson, *The Poems of Ossian &c.*, containing the Poetical Works of James Macpherson Esq. in Prose and Rhyme, ed Malcolm Laing, 2 vols (Edinburgh 1805; reprinted, intro. J. MacQueen, 1971)

Marilyn Butler, 'Romanticism in England' in *Romanticism in National Context*, eds Roy Porter & Mikuláš Teich (CUP, 1988)

Maurice Colgan, 'Ossian: Success or Failure for the Scottish Enlightenment?' in *Aberdeen and the Enlightenment*, eds Jennifer J. Carter & John H. Pittock (Aberdeen UP, 1987)

R.P. FitzGerald, 'The Style of Ossian', *Studies in Romanticism* 6 (1966), 22-33

Howard Gaskill (ed.), *Ossian Revisited* (EUP, 1991)

Ian Haywood, 'The Making of History: Historiography and Literary Forgery in the Eighteenth Century', *Literature and History* 9:2 (1988), 139-51

Jon Mee, '"Northern Antiquities": Bards, Druids and Ancient Liberties' in *Dangerous Enthusiasm: William Blake and the culture of radicalism in the 1790s* (OUP, 1992)

Peter T. Murphy, 'Fool's Gold: The Highland Treasures of Macpherson's Ossian' *ELH* 53:3 (1986), 567-91

Fiona Stafford, *The Sublime Savage: James Macpherson and the Poems of Ossian* (EUP, 1988)

Hugh Trevor-Roper, 'The Invention of Tradition: The Highland Tradition of Scotland' in *The Invention of Tradition* eds Eric Hobsbawm & Terence Ranger (CUP, 1983) 15-42

EDWARD YOUNG

Edward Young, Night Thoughts, ed. Stephen Cornford (CUP, 1989); for other texts see *The Works of the Author of "Night Thoughts"*. In Four Volumes, revised and corrected by himself (London, 1757).

C.C. Barfoot, '"A Paradise Unlost": Edward Young among the Stars' in *Between Dream and Reality: Essays on Utopia and Dystopia*, eds Dominic Baker-Smith & C.C. Barfoot (Amsterdam: Rodopi, 1987) 139-71

Werner Bronnimann, 'Edward Young's Estranged Readers' in *On Strangeness*, ed. Margaret Bridges (Tubingen, 1900) 73-84

Stephen Cox, *'The Stranger within Thee': concepts of self in late eighteenth-century literature* (Pittsburgh UP, 1980)

George Eliot, 'Worldiness and Other-Worldiness: the Poet Young', *Westminster Review* LXVII (1857); reprinted in *Essays of George Eliot*, ed. Thomas Pinney (London, 1963) 335-87

Northrop Frye, 'Towards Defining an Age of Sensibility', *ELH* 23 (1956), 144-52; reprinted in *Fables of Identity* (New York, 1963), 130-37

Martin Price, 'The Sublime Poem', *Yale Review* 58 (1968-9), 194-213

Cheryl Wanko, 'The Making of a Minor Poet: Edward Young and Literary Taxonomy', *English Studies* 72:4 (1991), 355-67

Merrill D. Whitburn, 'The Rhetoric of Otherworldliness in "Night Thoughts"', *Essays in Literature* 5 (1978), 163-74.

Mark Akenside

Mark Akenside was born in 1721, the son of a Presbyterian butcher in Newcastle-upon-Tyne: a leg maimed in a childhood accident with his father's cleaver served as a permanent reminder of his upbringing. He was educated at Newcastle Grammar School, excelling both in classical learning and precocious poetic output. His first notable piece, 'Hymn to Science', appeared in *The Gentleman's Magazine* in 1739 when he was seventeen, and large portions of his major work, *The Pleasures of Imagination*, may also have been composed during this period. The local dissenting community sponsored him to study for the ministry at Edinburgh University the following year, a scholarship refunded in full on his subsequent decision to transfer to medicine. He went on to qualify as Doctor of Physic at Leyden, presenting a highly regarded dissertation on the evolution of the human foetus.

In 1743, he returned from Germany with the manuscript of *The Pleasures of Imagination*, for which he demanded and received £120: the bookseller, Dodsley, consulted Pope who assured him 'this was no every-day writer'.[1] The poem was published in January 1744, and despite its abstruse topic and dense elaboration of argument received instant acclaim. It was quickly followed by *An Epistle to Curio*, an impressively sustained denunciation of William Pulteney for his defection to the Court Party; *Odes on Several Subjects*, notable chiefly for its introduction to a series of hitherto unknown classical metres into English verse; and the austere and somewhat forbidding *Hymn to the Naiads*.

Akenside's relative lack of professional success – three meagre years in Northampton, with little improvement on moving to Hampstead in 1747 – was attributed to the offence caused to potential clients by his outspoken libertarianism, what Johnson called his 'impetuous eagerness to subvert and confound, with little care what may be established' (*Lives* 3:412). This intemperate vein of inner-light Protestantism, interestingly comparable to Blake's amalgam of imagination and dissent, was not, however, to lead to similar impoverishment: the attachment of a wealthy patron, Jeremiah Dyson, proved sufficiently intense to support him with the lavish allowance of £300 per annum. In his final years, Akenside enjoyed the trappings of success: Fellow of the Royal Society in 1753; membership of the Royal Society of Physicians and honorary degree at Cambridge in 1754; and prestigious guest lecturer to the Royal Court of Medicine in 1755 and 1756. He became chief physician at Christs and St Thomas' Hospital, where he was renowned for his impatience and, at times, brutality towards his patients: one unfortunate invalid, too ill to swallow his prescribed medicine, was peremptorily discharged and died being carried off the premises.

An appointment as court physician on the accession of George III in 1761 led Akenside to abandon his previous radicalism. His writing also trailed off, though he still produced some encomiastic and exhortatory political verse, and various shorter pieces, including the impressively lapidary *Inscriptions*. The major project of his final years was a complete reworking of *The Pleasures of Imagination*, whose extravagant rhapsodic style now offended him. Revised versions of the first and second books appeared in 1757 and 1765; an unfinished third, on the struggles of Solon against the tyrant Pisistratus, and a fragment of a fourth on the origins of genius, were published after his death in 1770.

Akenside's work received lavish contemporary acclaim: even Johnson's often acerbic account acknowledges him 'in the general fabrication of his lines' to be 'perhaps superior to any other writer of blank verse' (*Lives* 3:417), and it is almost shocking to realize that this includes Milton. His reputation has now slumped, to the point where criticism feels entitled to treat him as no more than that most forlorn and despised of all literary phenomena: the representative figure. There are undoubtedly problems caused by his explicit adherence to a matrix of what now seems antiquated moral and aesthetic debate. The stated aims of the 1744 Design of *The Pleasures of Imagination* – 'to distinguish the imagination from other faculties', and 'to enumerate and exemplify the different species of pleasure' – may now, I freely admit, sound thoroughly unappealing. Perhaps the best way of approaching *The Pleasures of Imagination* is to compare its attempt 'To paint the finest features of the mind' (1:46) with *The Prelude*. Where Wordsworth seeks to detail 'the growth of a poet's mind' as a uniquely individual experience, Akenside invokes autobiographical detail to illustrate a more generally applicable schema. But his text is equally preoccupied with the processes of its own composition: as Mrs Barbauld, an early editor, remarked, 'Every step of the disquisition calls up objects of the most attractive kind, and Fancy is made as it were to hold a mirror to her own charms'.[2]

I would also make a strong historical claim for the importance of its central thematic concern: pleasure. During this period, the concept is both being secularized, detached from the Christian myth of temptation and fall, and used to sacramentalize the imagination, create a model of the mind in which the most intense human experiences occur in an aesthetic rather than a religious realm. Thus Akenside can confidently invoke a spirit of Beauty that 'Illumes the headstrong impulse of desire/ And sanctifies his [man's] choice' (1:363-4). *The Pleasures of Imagination* can be seen as the founder of a powerful tradition of agnostic hedonism, running through Keats via Pater through to Stevens (evident in such lines as 'The bloom of nectar'd fruitage ripe to sense' (1:367)).

The initial obstacle to a fuller appreciation is the low esteem in which the whole genre of the eighteenth-century verse treatise is currently held. The impressively unified sensibility of these panegyrists of science deserves

18

to be stressed.[3] Their 'embellishment' of a given topic shows no antagonism or envious distraction, but rather a gracious deference and a desire to assimilate; if their verse is at times prone to florid obsequiousness, it can also rise to a disciplined celebration of the collective human enterprise. For Akenside, *The Pleasures of Imagination* becomes something more: a means of divesting reason of its drab and penitential asceticism, and reconciling it with a jubilant celebration of pleasure, and thereby, to adapt a phrase from the 'Hymn to Science', 'To bless the lab'ring mind' (6). Technically, this synthesis can be explained as an enlargement of the role of imagination through the importation of a Platonic aesthetic of ideal forms – in particular, Beauty – into what remains a predominantly Lockean psychology.

More important than the formal argument, however, is the commingling of intellectual idiom allowed by the poem's 'open, pathetic, and figured stile' (Design, p.6). The initial sense of a paraphrasable treatise must be weighed against what Johnson called this 'luxuriance of expression':

> His images ... are forms fantastically lost under superfluity of dress ...
> The words are multiplied till the sense is hardly perceived; attention
> deserts the mind, and settles in the ear. The reader wanders through
> the gay diffusion, sometimes amazed and sometimes delighted, but
> after many turnings in the flowery labyrinth comes out as he went in.
> He remarked little and laid hold on nothing. (*Lives* 3:417)

Johnson tries to reduce this voluptuous thickening, through which the 'sense' can be 'hardly perceived', to a 'superfluity of dress', but the 'form' or 'image' of the referent, the origin, is now 'lost', hidden at the centre of a 'labyrinth' through which the reader 'wanders ... amazed'. The 'gay diffusion' ('his flow is smooth') is set against the moral imperative to 'remark' and 'lay hold', and resist at all costs the enticements of 'delight'. This is not, however, to come out with nothing. There's no difficulty in finding passages of immediate formal excellence: decorous, controlled, with a stately, though perhaps slightly over-deliberate, euphony, like a more firmly etched and less melodically delicate Collins. But Akenside's 'vagrant plume' (1:296) has considerably greater range than this. There is a breakdown of any firm subordination of illustration to argument, and a continual infiltration and expansion of the analytic within his 'free-flowing verse' (1:273), creating a realm of free play in which the 'amiable toil' (2:33) and the 'glad task' (2:67) of the 'sprightly joy' (1:232) may flourish.

The bulk of the selections are from the first version of *The Pleasures of Imagination*, by which Akenside's reputation must largely stand or fall. These emphasize his attempt to recoin the language of reason, but also include his impressive invocation of the Grecian heritage, the set-pieces of the soul's extra-terrestrial excursion and the progress of poetry towards 'Albion's happy shore' (2:44), and a selection of assorted (usually contradictory) theodicies. From the second version I have taken the opening invocation, a useful standard for comparison of early and late styles, an example of glacial Platonic ecstasy, and the final fragment on the origin of genius, an eloquent anticipation of and formative influence on the early books of *The Prelude*. Whig phillipic, one of the least appealing of all poetical genres, calls forth Akenside's least attractive manner, stiffly oracular and interminably loquacious. But there is one extremely fine poem among his political verse: *An Epistle to Curio*. Here Akenside's habitual abrasiveness gives a sense of personal grievance and betrayal to a formal public address: the effort of self-restraint implied by its elevated moral decorum becomes the standard by which Pulteney is to be judged and condemned. The poem splendidly carries off one of the rarest of rhetorical feats: a sustained display of principled invective.

Due credit should also be given to a related strain of a candid emotional pragmatism. Whereas the rakish cynicism of Prior, for example, is eminently compatible with polished sentimentality, Akenside's love poetry seems to opt out of the game altogether, speaking with unadorned directness about pain, resentment and resilience (something like an unfacetious Clough). Johnson commented of Akenside's shorter pieces: 'One bad ode may be suffered; but a number of them together make one sick' (*Life of Johnson* 2:164). Nevertheless I have put in a few samples: these tend to offer proto-Romantic themes in a rather colourless neoclassical diction, bardic inspiration in the third person, although the peculiar self-evacuation of the 'Ode to the Evening Star' proves an interesting exception. The ascetic impassivity of the elaborate mythological pantheon of the *Hymn to the Naiads*, and the effacement of personal voice before a communal and levelling cultural heritage in the *Inscriptions*, may perhaps be an acquired taste, but contrasts favourably with later, often tumid and opportunist, Romantic responses to the Greek revival: in this, as in many other aspects of his work, Akenside's disciplined fervour survives the comparison with his more illustrious successors surprisingly well.

Hymn to Science

Science! thou fair effusive ray
From the great source of mental Day,
    Free, generous, and refin'd!
Descend with all thy treasures fraught,
Illumine each bewilder'd thought,
    And bless my lab'ring mind.

But first with thy resistless light,
   Disperse those phantoms from my sight,
Those mimic shades of thee:
The scholiast's learning, sophist's cant,   10
The visionary bigot's rant,
   The monk's philosophy.

O! let thy powerful charms impart
The patient head, the candid heart,
   Devoted to thy sway;
Which no weak passions e'er mislead,
Which still with dauntless steps proceed
   Where Reason points the way.

Give me to learn such secret cause;
Let number's, figure's, motion's laws   20
   Reveal'd before me stand;
These to great Nature's scenes apply,
And round the globe, and thro' the sky,
   Disclose her working hand.

Next, to thy nobler search resign'd,
The busy, restless, human mind
   Thro' every maze pursue;
Detect Perception where it lies,
Catch the Ideas as they rise,
   And all their changes view.   30

Say from what simple springs began
The vast ambitious thoughts of man,
   Which range beyond controul,
Which seek Eternity to trace,
Dive thro' th' infinity of space,
   And strain to grasp The Whole.

Her secret stores let Memory tell,
Bid Fancy quit her fairy cell,
   In all her colours drest;
While prompt her sallies to controul,   40
Reason the judge, recalls the soul
   To truth's severest test.

Then launch thro' Being's wide extent;
Let the fair scale, with just ascent,
   And cautious steps, be trod;
And from the dead, corporeal mass,
Thro' each progressive order pass
   To Instinct, Reason, God.

There, Science! veil thy daring eye;
Nor dive too deep, nor soar too high,   50
   In that divine abyss;
To Faith content thy beams to lend,
Her hopes t'assure, her steps befriend
   And light her way to bliss.

Then downwards take thy flight agen,
Mix with the policies of men,
   And social nature's ties;
The plan, the genius of each state,
Its interest and its pow'rs relate,
   Its fortunes and its rise.   60

Thro' private life pursue thy course,
Trace every action to its source,
   And means and motives weigh:
Put tempers, passions, in the scale;
Mark what degrees in each prevail,
   And fix the doubtful sway.

That last best effort of thy skill,
To form the life, and rule the will,
   Propitious power! impart:
Teach me to cool my passion's fires,   70
Make me the judge of my desires,
   The master of my heart.

Raise me above the vulgar's breath,
Pursuit of fortune, fear of death,
   And all in life's that's mean.
Still true to reason be my plan,
Still let my actions speak the man,
   Thro' every various scene.

Hail! queen of manners, light of truth;
Hail! charm of age, and guide of youth;   80
   Sweet refuge of distress:
In business, thou! exact, polite;
Thou giv'st Retirement its delight,
   Prosperity its grace.

Of wealth, pow'r, freedom, thou! the cause;
Foundress of order, cities, laws,
   Of arts inventress, thou!
Without thee, what were human-kind?
How vast their wants, their thoughts how blind!
   Their joys how mean! how few!   90

Sun of the soul! thy beams unveil!
Let others spread the daring sail,
   On Fortune's faithless sea:
While undeluded, happier I
From the vain tumult timely fly,
   And sit in peace with Thee.

The Pleasures of Imagination

BOOK I

With what attractive charms this goodly frame
Of nature touches the consenting hearts
Of mortal men; and what the pleasing stores
Which beauteous imitation thence derives
To deck the poet's, or the painter's toil;
My verse unfolds. Attend, ye gentle powers
Of musical delight! and while I sing
Your gifts, your honours, dance around my strain.
Thou, smiling queen of every tuneful breast,
Indulgent Fancy! from the tuneful banks   10
Of Avon, whence thy rosy fingers cull
Fresh flowers and dews to sprinkle on the turf
Where Shakespeare lies, be present: and with thee
Let Fiction come, upon her vagrant wings
Wafting ten thousand colours thro' the air,
Which, by the glances of her magic eye,
She blends and shifts at will, thro' countless forms,
Her wild creation. Goddess of the lyre
Which rules the accents of the moving sphere,
Wilt thou, eternal Harmony! descend,   20
And join this festive train? for with thee comes
The guide, the guardian of their lovely sports,
Majestic Truth; and where Truth deigns to come,
Her sister Liberty will not be far.
Be present all ye Genii, who conduct
The wand'ring footsteps of the youthful bard,
New to your springs and shades: who touch his ear
With finer sounds; who heighten to his eye
The bloom of Nature, and before him turn
The gayest, happiest attitude of things.   30

Oft have the laws of each poetic strain
The critic-verse employed; yet still unsung
Lay this prime subject, though importing most

24

A poet's name: for fruitless is th' attempt,
By dull obedience and by creeping toil
Obscure to conquer the severe ascent
Of high Parnassus. Nature's kindling breath
Must fire the chosen genius; nature's hand
Must string his nerves, and imp his eagle-wings
Impatient of the painful steep, to soar   40
High as the summit: there to breathe at large
Aethereal air: with bards and sages old,
Immortal sons of praise. These flatt'ring scenes,
To this neglected labour court my song;
Yet not unconscious what a doubtful task
To paint the finest features of the mind,
And to most subtle and mysterious things
Give colour, strength, and motion. But the love
Of nature and the muses bids explore,
Thro' secret paths erewhile untrod by man,   50
The fair poetic region, to detect
Untasted springs, to drink inspiring draughts;
And shade my temples with unfading flowers
Cull'd from the laureate vale's profound recess,
Where never poet gain'd a wreath before.

From heav'n my strains begin: from heav'n descends
The flame of genius to the human breast,
And love and beauty, and poetic joy
And inspiration. Ere the radiant sun
Sprang from the east, or 'mid the vault of night   60
The moon suspended her serener lamp;
Ere mountains, woods, or streams adorn'd the globe,
Or wisdom taught the sons of men her lore;
Then liv'd th' almighty One: then deep-retir'd
In his unfathom'd essence, view'd the forms,
The forms eternal of created things;
The radiant sun, the moon's nocturnal lamp,
The mountains, woods and streams, the rolling globe,
And wisdom's mien celestial. From the first

25

Of days, on them his love divine he fix'd,   70
His admiration: till in time compleat
What he admir'd and lov'd, his vital smile
Unfolded into being. Hence the breath
Of life informing each organic frame,
Hence the green earth, and wild resounding waves;
Hence light and shade alternate; warmth and cold;
And clear autumnal skies and vernal showers,
And all the fair variety of things.

                              *

For as old Memnon's image, long renowned
By fabling Nilus, to the quivering touch   110
Of Titan's ray, with each repulsive string
Consenting, sounded thro' the warbling air
Unbidden strains; ev'n so did Nature's hand
To certain species of external things,
Attune the finer organs of the mind:
So the glad impulse of congenial powers,
Or of sweet sound, or fair proportion'd form,
The grace of motion, or the bloom of light,
Thrills thro' imagination's tender frame,
From nerve to nerve: all naked and alive   120
They catch the spreading rays: till now the soul
At length discloses every tuneful spring,
To the harmonous movement from without,
Responsive. Then the inexpressive strain
Diffuses its inchantment...

                              *

Say, why was man so eminently rais'd
Amid the vast creation; why ordain'd
Thro' life and death to dart his piercing eye,
With thoughts beyond the limit of his frame;
But that the omnipotent might send him forth

In sight of mortal and immortal powers,
As on a boundless theatre, to run
The great career of justice; to exalt
His gen'rous aim to all diviner deeds;
To chase each partial purpose from his breast;   160
And thro' the mists of passion and of sense,
And thro' the tossing tide of chance and pain,
To hold his course unfalt'ring, while the voice
Of truth and nature, up the steep ascent
Of nature, calls him to his high reward,
Th' applauding smile of Heaven? else wherefore burns
In mortal bosoms this unquenched hope,
That breaths from day to day sublimer things,
And mocks possession? wherefore darts the mind,
With such resistless ardor to imbrace   170
Majestic forms; impatient to be free,
Spurning the gross controul of wilful might;
Proud of the strong contention of her toils;
Proud to be daring? who but rather turns
To heaven's broad fire his unconstrained view,
Than to the glimm'ring of a waxen flame?
Who that, from Alpine heights, his lab'ring eye
Shoots round the wide horizon, to survey
Nilus or Ganges rowling his bright wave
Thro' mountains, plains, thro' empires black with shade   180
And continents of sand; will turn his gaze
To mark the windings of a scanty rill
That murmurs at his feet? The high-born soul
Disdains to rest her heav'n aspiring wing
Beneath its native quarry. Tir'd of earth
And this diurnal scene, she springs aloft
Thro' fields of air; pursues the flying storm;
Rides on the vollied lightning thro' the heav'ns;
Or, yok'd with whirlwinds and the northern blast,
Sweeps the long tract of day. Then high she soars   190
The blue profound, and hovering round the sun
Beholds him pouring the redundant stream

Of light; beholds his unrelenting sway
Bend the reluctant planets to absolve
The fated rounds of Time. Thence far effus'd
She darts her swiftness up the long career
Of devious comets; thro' its burning signs
Exulting measures the perennial wheel
Of nature, and looks back on all the stars,
Whose blended light, as with a milky zone,   200
Invests the orient. Now amaz'd she views
Th' empyreal waste, where happy spirits hold
Beyond this concave heav'n, their calm abode;
And fields of radiance, whose unfading light
Has travell'd the profound six thousand years,
Nor yet arrives in sight of mortal things.
Ev'n on the barriers of the world untir'd
She meditates the eternal depth below;
Till half recoiling, down the headlong steep
She plunges; soon o'erwhelmed and swallowed up   210
In that immense of being. There her hopes
Rest at the fated goal. For from the birth
Of mortal man, the sovran Maker said,
That not in humble nor in brief delight,
Not in the fading echoes of renown,
Power's purple robes, nor pleasure's flowery lap,
The soul should find enjoyment: but from these
Turning disdainful to an equal good,
Thro' all the ascent of things inlarge her view,
Till every bound at length should disappear,   220
And infinite perfection close the scene.

*

But lo! disclos'd in all her smiling pomp,
Where Beauty onward moving claims the verse
Her charms inspire: the freely-flowing verse
In thy immortal praise, O form divine,
Smooths her mellifluent stream. Thee, Beauty, thee,

The regal dome, and thy enlivening ray
The mossy roofs adore: thou, better sun!
For ever beamest on the inchanted heart
Love, and harmonious wonder, and delight
Poetic. Brightest progeny of heav'n!   280
How shall I trace thy features? where select
The roseate hues to emulate thy bloom?
Haste then, my song, thro' nature's wide expanse,
Haste then, and gather all her comeliest wealth,
Whate'er bright spoils the florid earth contains,
Whate'er the waters, or the liquid air,
To deck thy lovely labour. Wilt thou fly
With laughing autumn to th' Atlantic isles,
And range with him the Hesperian field, and see,
Where'er his fingers touch the fruitful grove,   290
The branches shoot with gold; where'er his step
Marks the glad soil, the tender clusters grow
With purple ripeness, and invest each hill
As with the blushes of an evening sky?
Or wilt thou rather stoop thy vagrant plume,
Where gliding thro' his daugher's honour'd shades,
The smooth Peneus from his glassy flood
Reflects purpureal Tempe's pleasant scene?

*

    Ye smiling band
Of youths and virgins, who thro' all the maze
Of young desire with rival steps pursue
This charm of beauty; if the pleasing toil
Can yield a moment's respite, hither turn
Your favourable ear, and trust my words.   340
I do not mean to wake the gloomy form
Of superstition drest in wisdom's garb,
To damp your tender hopes; I do not mean
To bid the jealous thunderer fire the heavens,
Or shapes infernal rend the groaning earth

To fright you from your joys: my cheerful song
With better omens calls you to the field,
Pleas'd with your generous ardour in the chace,
And warm like you. Then tell me, for ye know,
Does beauty ever deign to dwell where health   350
And active use are strangers? Is her charm
Confessed in aught, whose most peculiar ends
Are lame and fruitless? Or did nature mean
This pleasing call the herald of a lie;
To hide the shame of discord and disease,
And catch with fair hypocrisy the heart
Of idle faith? O no! with better cares
The indulgent mother, conscious how infirm
Her offspring tread the paths of good and ill,
By this illustrious image, in each kind   360
Still most illustrious where the object holds
Its native powers most perfect, she by this
Illumes the headstrong impulse of desire, headlong
And sanctifies his choice The generous glebe
Whose bosom smiles with verdure, the clear tract
Of streams delicious to the thirsty soul,
The bloom of nectar'd fruitage ripe to sense,
And every charm of animated things,
Are only pledges of a state sincere,
Th' integrity and order of their frame,   370
When all is well within, and every end
Accomplish'd. Thus was beauty sent from heav'n,
The lovely ministress of truth and good
In this dark world: for truth and good are one,
And beauty dwells in them, and they in her,
With like participation.

*

    And if the gracious pow'r
Who first awakened my untutor'd song,
Will to my invocation breath anew

30

The tuneful spirit; then thro' all our paths,
Ne'er shall the sound of this devoted lyre
Be wanting, whether on the rosy mead,
When summer smiles, to warn the melting heart
Of luxury's allurement; whether firm
Against the torrent and the stubborn hill
To urge bold virtue's unremitted nerve,   430
And wake the strong divinity of soul
That conquers chance and fate; or whether struck
For sounds of triumph, to proclaim her toils
Upon the lofty summit, round her brow
To twine the wreath of incorruptive praise;
To trace her hallow'd light thro' future worlds,
And bless heav'n's image in the heart of man.
    Thus with faithful aim have we presum'd,
Adventurous, to delineate nature's form;
Whether in vast, majestic pomp array'd,   440
Or drest for pleasing wonder, or serene
In beauty's rosy smile. It now remains,
Thro' various being's fair proportion'd scale,
To trace the rising lustre of her charms,
From their first twilight, shining forth at length
To full meridian splendour. Of degree
The least and lowliest, in th' effusive warmth
Of colours mingling with a random blaze,
Doth beauty dwell. Then higher in the line
And variation of determin'd shape,   450
Where truth's eternal measures mark the bound
Of circle, cube, or sphere. The third ascent
Unites the varied symmetry of parts
With colour's bland allurement; as the pearl
Shines in the concave of its azure bed,
And painted shells indent their speckled wreath.
Then more attractive rise the blooming forms
Thro' which the breath of nature has infus'd
Her genial power to draw with pregnant veins
Nutritious moisture from the bounteous earth,   460

31

In fruit and seed prolific: thus the flow'rs
Their purple honours with the spring resume;
And such the stately tree which autumn bends
With blushing treasures. But more lovely still
Is nature's charm, where to the full consent
Of complicated members, to the bloom
Of colour, and the vital change of growth,
Life's holy flame and piercing sense are given,
And active motion speaks the temper'd soul:
So moves the bird of Juno; so the steed   470
With rival ardour beats the dusty plain,
And faithful dogs with eager airs of joy
Salute their fellows. Thus doth beauty dwell
There most conspicuous, ev'n in outward shape,
Where dawns the high expression of a mind:
By steps conducting our enraptur'd search
To that eternal origin, whose pow'r,
Thro' all th' unbounded symmetry of things,
Like rays effulging from the parent sun,
This endless mixture of her charms diffus'd.   480
Mind, mind alone, bear witness earth and heav'n!
The living fountains in itself contains,
Of beauteous and sublime . . .

*

Once more search, undismay'd, the dark profound
Where nature works in secret; view the beds
Of mineral treasure, and th' eternal vault
That bounds the hoary ocean, trace the forms
Of atoms moving with incessant change
Their elemental round; behold the seeds
Of being, and the energy of life
Kindling the mass with ever-active flame:
Then to the secrets of the working mind   520
Attentive turn; from dim oblivion call
Her fleet, ideal band; and bid them, go!

32

Break thro' time's barrier, and o'ertake the hour
That saw the heavens created: then declare
If aught were found in those external scenes
To move thy wonder now. For what were all
The forms which brute, unconscious matter wears,
Greatness of bulk, or symmetry of parts?
Not reaching to the heart, soon feeble grows
The superficial impulse; dull their charms,   530
And satiate soon, and pall the languid eye.
Not so the moral species...

*

Genius of antient Greece! whose faithful steps
Well pleas'd I follow thro' the sacred paths
Of nature and of science; nurse divine
Of all heroic deeds and fair desires!   570
O! let the breath of thy extended praise
Inspire my kindling bosom to the height
Of this untempted theme. Nor be my thoughts
Presumptuous counted, if, amid the calm
That soothes the vernal evening into smiles,
I steal impatient from the sordid haunts
Of strife and low ambition, to attend
Thy sacred presence in the sylvan shade,
By their malignant footsteps ne'er profan'd.
Descend, propitious! to my favour'd eye;   580
Such in thy mien, thy warm, exalted air,
As when the Persian tyrant, foil'd and stung
With shame and desperation, gnash'd his teeth
To see thee rend the pageants of his throne;
And at the lightning of thy lifted spear
Crouch'd like a slave. Bring all thy martial spoils,
Thy palms, thy laurels, thy triumphal songs,
Thy smiling band of arts, thy godlike sires
Of civil wisdom, thy heroic youth
Warm from the schools of glory. Guide my way   590

Thro' fair Lyceum's walk, the green retreats
Of Academus, and the thymy vale,
Where oft inchanted with Socratic sounds,
Illusus pure devolv'd his tuneful stream
In gentler murmurs. From the blooming store
Of these auspicious fields, may I unblam'd
Transplant some living blossoms to adorn
My native clime: while far above the flight
Of fancy's plume aspiring, I unlock
The springs of ancient wisdom; while I join   600
Thy name, thrice honoured! with the immortal praise
Of nature; while to my compatriot youth
I point the high example of thy sons,
And tune to Attic themes the British lyre.

BOOK II

When shall the laurel and the vocal string
Resume their honours? When shall we behold
The tuneful tongue, the Promethean hand
Aspire to antient praise? Alas! how faint,
How slow the dawn of beauty and of truth
Breaks the reluctant shades of gothic night
Which yet involve the nations! Long they groan'd
Beneath the furies of rapacious force;
Oft as the gloomy north, with iron swarms
Tempestuous pouring from her frozen caves,   10
Blasted th' Italian shore, and swept the works
Of liberty and wisdom down the gulph
Of all-devouring night. As long immur'd
In noontide darkness by the glimm'ring lamp,
Each muse and each fair science pined away
The sordid hours: while foul, barbarian hands
Their mysteries profan'd, unstrung the lyre
And chain'd the soaring pinion down to earth.
At last the muses rose, and spurn'd their bonds,
And, wildly warbling, scatter'd as they flew,   20

34

Their blooming wreaths from fair Valclusa's bow'rs
To Arno's myrtle border and the shore
Of soft Parthenope. But still the rage
Of dire ambition and gigantic pow'r,
From publick aims and from the busy walk
Of civil commerce, drove the bolder train
Of penetrating science to the cells,
Where studious ease consumes the silent hour,
In shadowy searches, and unfruitful care.
Thus from their guardians torn, the tender arts   30
Of mimic fancy and harmonious joy,
To priestly domination and the lust
Of lawless courts, their amiable toil
For three inglorious ages have resign'd,
In vain reluctant: and Torquato's tongue
Was tun'd for slavish paeans at the throne
Of tinsel pomp: and Raphael's magic hand
Effus'd its fair creation to inchant
The fond adoring herd in Latian fanes
To blind belief; while on their prostrate necks   40
The sable tyrant plants his heel secure.
But now, behold! the radiant aera dawns,
When freedom's ample fabric, fixed at length
For endless years on Albion's happy shore
In full proportion, once more shall extend
To all the kindred pow'rs of social bliss
A common mansion, a parental roof.
There shall the virtues, there shall wisdom's train,
Their long-lost friends rejoining, as of old,
Embrace the smiling family of arts,   50
The muses and the graces. Then no more
Shall vice, distracting their delicious gifts
To aims abhorr'd, with high distaste and scorn
Turn from their charms the philosophic eye,
The patriot-bosom: then no more the paths
Of publick care or intellectual toil
Alone by footsteps haughty and severe

In gloomy state be trod: th' harmonious muse
And her persuasive sisters then shall plant
Their shelt'ring laurels o'er the bleak ascent,   60
And scatter flowers along the rugged way.
Armed with the lyre, already have we dar'd
To pierce divine philosophy's retreats,
And teach the muse her lore; already strove
Their long divided honours to unite,
While temp'ring this deep argument we sang
Of truth and beauty...

*

Or shall I mention, where coelestial truth
Her awful light discloses, to bestow
A more majestic pomp on beauty's frame?
For man loves knowledge, and the beams of truth   100
More welcome touch his understanding's eye,
Than all the blandishments of sound, his ear,
Than all of taste his tongue. Nor ever yet
The melting rainbow's vernal-tinctur'd hues
To me have shown so pleasing, as when first
The hand of science pointed out the path
In which the sun-beams gleaming from the west
Fall on the wat'ry cloud, whose darksome veil
Involves the orient; and that trickling shower
Piercing thro' ev'ry crystalline convex   110
Of clust'ring dewdrops to their flight oppos'd,
Recoil at length where concave all behind
Th' internal surface of each glassy orb
Repells their forward passage into air;
That thence direct they seek the radiant goal
From which their course began; and, as they strike
In diff'rent lines the gazer's obvious eye,
Assume a diff'rent lustre, thro' the brede
Of colours changing from the splendid rose
To the pale violet's dejected hue.   120

*

What, when to raise the meditated scene,
The flame of passion, thro' the struggling soul
Deep-kindled, shows across that sudden blaze
The object of its rapture, vast of size,
With fiercer colours, and a night of shade?   140
What? like a storm from their capacious bed
The sounding seas o'erwhelming, when the might
Of these eruptions, working from the depth
Of man's strong apprehension, shakes his frame
Ev'n to the base; from every naked sense
Of pain or pleasure dissipating all
Opinion's feeble cov'rings, and the veil
Spun from the cobweb-fashion of the times
To hide the feeling heart? Then nature speaks
Her genuine language, and the words of men,   150
Big with the very motion of their souls,
Declare with what accumulated force,
Th' impetuous nerve of passion urges on
The native weight and energy of things.

*

Yet by immense benignity inclin'd
To spread around him that primaeval joy
Which fill'd himself, he rais'd his plastic arm,
And sounded thro' the hollow depth of space
The strong, creative mandate. Strait arose   315
These heavenly orbs, the glad abodes of life
Effusive kindled by his breath divine
Thro' endless forms of being...
                    ...Nor content
By one exertion of creative pow'r
His goodness to reveal; thro' every age,
Thro' every moment up the tract of time,   340
His parent-hand with ever-new increase
Of happiness and virtue has adorn'd
The vast harmonious frame: his parent-hand

37

From the mute shell-fish gasping on the shore,
To men, to angels, to celestial minds
For ever leads the generations on
To higher scenes of being; while supply'd
From day to day with his enlivening breath,
Inferior orders in succession rise
To fill the void below. As flame ascends,   350
As bodies to their proper centre move,
As the pois'd ocean to the attracting moon
Obedient swells, and every headlong stream
Devolves its winding waters to the main;
So all things which have life aspire to God,
The sun of being, boundless, unimpair'd,
Center of souls! Nor does the faithful voice
Of Nature cease to prompt their eager steps
Aright; nor is the care of Heaven withheld
From granting to the task proportion'd aid;   360
That in their stations all may persevere
To climb th' ascent of being, and approach
For ever nearer to the life divine.

*

Let not this headlong terror quite o'erwhelm
Thy scatter'd powers; nor fatal deem the rage
Of this tormentor, nor his proud assault,
While I am here to vindicate thy toil,   580
Above the generous question of thy arm.
Brave by thy fears and in thy weakness strong,
This hour he triumphs: but confront his might,
And dare him to the combat, then with ease
Disarm'd and quell'd, his fierceness he resigns
To bondage and to scorn: while thus inur'd
By watchful danger, by unceasing toil,
The immortal mind, superior to his fate,
Amid the outrage of external things,
Firm as the solid base of this great world,   590

38

Rests on his own foundations. Blow, ye winds!
Ye waves! ye thunders! roll your tempest on;
Shake, ye old pillars of the marble sky!
Till all its orbs and all its worlds of fire
Be loosen'd from their seats; yet still serene
The unconquer'd mind looks down upon the wreck;
And ever stronger as the storms advance,
Firm thro' the closing ruin holds his way,
Where Nature calls him to the destin'd goal.

*

Say; when the prospect blackens on thy view,
When rooted from the base, heroic states
Mourn in the dust and tremble at the frown
Of curst ambition; when the pious band
Of youths who fought for freedom and their sires,
Lie side by side in gore; when ruffian pride
Usurps the throne of justice, turns the pomp
Of public power, the majesty of rule,   730
The sword, the laurel, and the purple robe,
To slavish empty pageants, to adorn
A tyrant's walk, and glitter in the eyes
Of such as bow the knee; when honour'd urns
Of patriots and of chiefs, the awful bust
And storied arch, to glut the coward-rage
Of regal envy, strew the public way
With hallow'd ruins; when the muse's haunt,
The marble porch where wisdom wont to talk
With Socrates or Tully, hears no more,   740
Save the hoarse jargon of contentious monks,
Or of female superstition's midnight prayer;
When ruthless rapine from the hand of time
Tears the destroying scythe, with surer blow
To sweep the works of glory from their base;
Till desolation o'er the grass-grown street
Expands his raven-wings, and up the wall,

Where senates once the price of monarchs doom'd,
Hisses the gliding snake thro' hoary weeds
That clasp the mouldering column...   750

BOOK III

Such are the various aspects of the mind –
Some heavenly genius, whose unclouded thoughts
Attain that secret harmony which blends   280
Th' aetherial spirit with its mold of clay;
O! teach me to reveal the grateful charm
That searchless nature o'er the sense of man
Diffuses, to behold, in lifeless things,
The inexpressive semblance of himself,
Of thought and passion. Mark the sable woods
That shade sublime yon mountain's nodding brow;
With what religious awe the solemn scene
Commands your steps! as if the reverend form
Of Minos or of Numa should forsake   290
Th' Elysian seats, and down th' imbowering glade
Move to your pausing eye! Behold th' expanse
Of yon gay landscape, where the silver clouds
Flit o'er the heav'ns before the sprightly breeze:
Now their gray cincture skirts the doubtful sun;
Now streams of splendor, thro' th' opening veil
Effulgent, sweep from off the gilded lawn
Th' aerial shadows; on the curling brook,
And on the shady margin's quivering leaves
With quickest lustre glancing; While you view   300
The prospect, say, within your cheerful breast
Plays not the lively sense of winning mirth
With clouds and sun-shine chequer'd, while the round
Of social converse, to th' inspiring tongue
Of some gay nymph amid her subject-train,
Moves all obsequious? Whence is this effect,
This kindred power of such discordant things?
Or flows their semblance from that mystic tone

40

To which the new-born mind's harmonious powers
At first were strung? Or rather from the links   310
Which artful custom twines around her frame?

*

By these mysterious ties, the busy power
Of memory her ideal train preserves
Intire; or when they would elude her watch,   350
Reclaims their fleeting footsteps from the waste
Of dark oblivion; thus collecting all
The various forms of being to present,
Before the curious aim of mimic art,
Their largest choice: like spring's unfolded blooms
Exhaling sweetness, that the skilful bee
May taste at will, from their selected spoils
To work her dulcet food. For not th' expanse
Of living lakes in summer's noontide calm,
Reflects the bord'ring shade, and sun-bright heav'ns   360
With fairer semblance; not the sculptur'd gold
More faithful keeps the graver's lively trace,
Than he whose birth the sister-pow'rs of art
Propitious view'd, and from his genial star
Shed influence to the seeds of fancy kind;
Than his attemper'd bosom must preserve
The seal of nature. There alone unchang'd,
Her form remains. The balmy walks of May
There breathe perennial sweets, the trembling chord
Resounds for ever in th' abstracted ear,   370
Melodious: and the virgin's radiant eye,
Superior to disease, to grief, and time,
Shines with unbating lustre. Thus at length
Endow'd with all that nature can bestow,
The child of fancy oft in silence bends
O'er these mixt treasures of his pregnant breast,
With conscious pride. From them he oft resolves
To frame he knows not what excelling things;

41

And win he knows not what sublime reward
Of praise and wonder. By degrees, the mind   380
Feels her young nerves dilate: the plastic powers
Labour for action: blind emotions heave
His bosom; and with loveliest frenzy caught,
From earth to heav'n he rolls his daring eye,
From heav'n to earth. Anon ten thousand shapes,
Like spectres trooping to the wisard's call,
Flit swift before him. From the womb of earth,
From ocean's bed they come: th' eternal heavens
Disclose their splendors, and the dark abyss
Pours out her births unknown. With fixed gaze   390
He marks the rising phantoms. Now compares
Their diff'rent forms, now blends them, now divides;
Enlarges and extentuates by turns;
Opposes, ranges in fantastic bands,
And infinitely varies. Hither now,
Now thither fluctuates his inconstant aim,
With endless choice perplex'd. At length his plan
Begins to open. Lucid order dawns;
And as from chaos old the jarring seeds
Of nature at the voice divine repair'd   400
Each to its place, till rosy earth unveil'd
Her fragrant bosom, and the joyful sun
Sprung up the blue serene: by swift degrees
Thus disentangled his entire design
Emerges. Colours mingle, features join,
And lines converge: the fainter parts retire;
The fairer eminent in light advance;
And every image on its neighbour smiles.
Awhile he stands, and with a father's joy
Contemplates. Then with Promethean art   410
Into its proper vehicle he breathes
The fair conception; which, imbodied thus,
And permanent, becomes to eyes or ears
An object ascertain'd: while thus inform'd,
The various organs of his mimic skill,

42

The consonance of sounds, the featured rock,
The shadowy picture and impassion'd verse,
Beyond their proper powers attract the soul
By that expressive semblance, while in sight
Of nature's great original we scan   420
The lively child of art; while line by line,
And feature after feature we refer
To that sublime exemplar whence it stole
Those animating charms. Thus beauty's palm
Betwixt them wav'ring hangs: applauding love
Doubts where to choose; and mortal man aspires
To tempt creative praise.

*

By what fine ties hath God connected things
When present in the mind, which in themselves
Have no connexion? Sure the rising sun,
O'er the caerulean convex of the sea,
With equal brightness and with equal warmth
Might rowl his fiery orb; nor yet the soul
Thus feel her frame expanded, and her pow'rs
Exulting in the splendor she beholds;
Like a young conqueror moving thro' the pomp   470
Of some triumphal day. When join'd at eve,
Soft-murm'ring streams and gales of gentlest breath
Melodious Philomela's wakeful strain
Attemper, could not man's discerning ear
Thro' all its tones the sympathy pursue;
Nor yet this breath divine of nameless joy
Steal thro' his veins and fan th' awakened heart,
Mild as the breeze, yet rapt'rous as the song?

*

Oh! blest of heav'n, whom not the languid songs
Of luxury, the siren! not the bribes

Of sordid wealth, nor all the gaudy spoils   570
Of pageant honour can seduce to leave
Those ever-blooming sweets, which from the store
Of nature fair imagination culls
To charm the inlivened soul! What tho' not all
Of mortal offspring can attain the heights
Of envied life; though only few possess
Patrician treasures or imperial state;
Yet nature's care, to all her children just,
With richer treasures and an ampler state,
Endows at large whatever happy man   580
Will deign to use them. His the city's pomp,
The rural honours his. Whate'er adorns
The princely dome, the column and the arch,
The breathing marbles and the sculptur'd gold,
Beyond the proud possessor's narrow claim,
His tuneful breast enjoys. For him, the spring
Distills her dews, and from the silken gem
Its lucid leaves unfolds: for him, the hand
Of autumn tinges every fertile branch
With blooming gold and blushes like the morn.   590
Each passing hour sheds tribute from her wings;
And still new beauties meet his lonely walk,
And loves unfelt attract him. Not a breeze
Flies o'er the meadow, not a cloud imbibes
The setting sun's effulgence, not a strain
From all the tenants of the warbling shade
Ascends, but whence his bosom can partake
Fresh pleasure, unreprov'd. Nor thence partakes
Fresh pleasure only: for th' attentive mind,
By this harmonious action on her pow'rs   600
Becomes herself harmonious: wont so oft
In outward things to meditate the charm
Of sacred order, soon she seeks at home
To find a kindred order, to exert
Within herself this elegance of love,
This fair-inspir'd delight: her temper'd pow'rs

44

Refine at length, and every passion wears
A chaster, milder, more attractive mien.
But if to ampler prospects, if to gaze
On nature's form, where, negligent of all   610
These lesser graces, she assumes the port
Of that eternal majesty that weigh'd
The world's foundations, if to these the mind
Exalt her daring eye, then mightier far
Will be the change, and nobler. Would the forms
Of servile custom cramp her gen'rous powers?
Would sordid policies, the barb'rous growth
Of ignorance and rapine, bow her down
To tame pursuits, to indolence and fear?
Lo! she appeals to nature, to the winds   620
And rowling waves, the sun's unwearied course,
The elements and seasons: all declare
For what th' eternal maker has ordain'd
The powers of man: we feel within ourselves
His energy divine: he tells the heart
He meant, he made us to behold and love
What he beholds and loves, the general orb
Of life and being; to be great like him,
Beneficent and active. Thus the men
Whom nature's works can charm, with God himself   630
Hold converse; grow familiar, day by day,
With his conceptions, act upon his plan;
And form to his, the relish of their souls.

An Epistle to Curio

Thrice has the spring beheld thy faded Fame,
And the fourth Winter rises on thy Shame,
Since I exulting grasp'd the votive Shell,
In Sounds of Triumph all thy Praise to tell;
Blest could my Skill through Ages make thee shine,
And proud to mix my Memory with thine.
But now the Cause that wak'd my Song before,
With Praise, with Triumph, crowns the Toil no more.
If to the glorious Man, whose faithful Cares,
Nor quell'd by Malice, nor relax'd by Years,   10
Had aw'd Ambition's wild audacious Hate,
And dragg'd at length Corruption to her Fate;
If every Tongue its large Applauses ow'd,
And well-earn'd Laurels every Muse bestow'd,
If public Justice urg'd the high Reward,
And Freedom smil'd on the devoted Bard;
Say then, to him whose Levity or Lust
Laid all a People's gen'rous Hopes in Dust;
Who taught Ambition firmer Heights of Pow'r,
And sav'd Corruption at her Hopeless hour;   20
Does not each Tongue its Execrations owe?
Shall not each Muse a Wreath of Shame bestow?
And public Justice sanctify th' Award?
And Freedom's Hand protect th' impartial Bard?

Yet long reluctant I forbore thy Name,
Long watch'd thy Virtue like a dying Flame,
Hung o'er each glimm'ring Spark with anxious Eyes,
And wish'd and hop'd the Light again would rise.
But since thy Guilt still more intire appears,
Since no Art hides, no Supposition clears;   30
Since vengeful Slander now too sinks her Blast,
And the first Rage of Party-hate is past;
Calm as the Judge of Truth, at length I come
To weigh thy Merits, and pronounce thy Doom:
So may my Trust from all Reproach be free,

46

And Earth and Time confirm the fair decree.
    There are who say they view'd without Amaze
The sad Reverse of all thy former Praise:
That thro' the Pageants of a Patriot's Name,
They pierc'd the Foulness of thy secret Aim;   40
Or deem'd thy Arm exalted but to throw
The public Thunder on a private Foe.
But I, whose Soul consented to thy Cause,
Who felt thy Genius stamp its own Applause,
Who saw the Spirits of each glorious Age
Move in thy Bosom, and direct thy Rage;
I scorn'd th' ungenerous Gloss of slavish Minds,
The Owl-ey'd race, whom Virtue's Lustre blinds.
Spite of the Learned in the ways of Vice,
And all who prove that each Man has his Price,   50
I still believ'd thy end was just and free;
And yet, ev'n yet believe it – spite of thee.
Ev'n tho' thy Mouth impure has dar'd disclaim,
Urg'd by the wretched Impotence of Shame,
Whatever filial Cares thy Zeal has paid
To Laws infirm, and Liberty decay'd;
Has begg'd Ambition to forgive the Show;
Has told Corruption thou wert ne'er her Foe;
Has boasted in the Country's awful Ear,
Her gross Delusion when she held thee dear;   60
How tame she follow'd thy tempestuous Call,
And heard thy pompous Tales, and trusted all –
Rise from your sad Abodes, ye Curst of old
For Laws subverted, and for Cities sold!
Paint all the noblest Trophies of your Guilt,
The Oaths you perjur'd and the Blood you spilt;
Yet must you one untempted Vileness own,
One dreadful Palm reserv'd for him alone;
With studied Arts his Country's Praise to spurn,
To beg the Infamy he did not earn,   70
To challenge Hate when Honour was his due,
And plead his Crimes when all his Virtue knew.

Do Robes of State the guarded Heart inclose
From each fair Feeling human Nature knows?
Can pompous Titles stun the inchant'd Ear
To all that Reason, all that Sense would hear?
Else couldst thou e'er desert thy sacred Post,
In such unthankful Baseness to be lost?
Else couldst thou wed the Emptiness of Vice,
And yield thy Glories at an Idiot's Price? 80

*

O lost, alike to Action and Repose!
Unknown, unpitied in the worst of Woes!
With all that conscious, undissembled Pride,
Sold to the Insults of a Foe defy'd! 170
With all that Habit of familiar Fame,
Doom'd to exhaust the Dregs of Life in Shame!
The sole sad Refuge of thy baffled Art,
To act a Statesman's dull, exploded Part . . .

*

O long rever'd and late resign'd to Shame!
If this uncourtly Page thy Notice claim 220
When the loud Cares of Business are withdrawn,
Nor well-drest Beggars round thy Footsteps fawn;
In that still, thoughtful, solitary Hour,
When Truth exerts her unresisted Pow'r,
Breaks the false Optic ting'd with Fortune's Glare,
Unlocks the Breast, and lays the Passions bare;
Then turn thy Eyes on that important Scene,
And ask thyself – if all be well within.
Where is the Heart-felt Worth and Weight of Soul,
Where the known Dignity, the Stamp of Awe, 230
Which, half-abash'd, the Proud and Venal saw?
Where the calm Triumphs of an honest Cause?
Where the delightful Taste of just Applause?

Where the strong Reason, the commanding Tongue,
On which the Senate fir'd or trembling hung?
All vanish'd, all are sold – And in their Room,
Couch'd in thy Bosom's deep, distracted Gloom,
See the pale Form of barb'rous Grandeur dwell,
Like some grim Idol in a Sorcerer's Cell!
To her in Chains thy Dignity was led;   240
At her polluted Shrine thy Honour bled;
With blasted Weeds thy awful Brow she crown'd,
Thy pow'rful Tongue with poison'd Philters bound,
That baffled Reason straight indignant flew,
And fair Persuasion from her seat withdrew:
For now no longer Truth supports thy Cause;
No longer Glory prompts thee to Applause;
No longer Virtue breathing in thy Breast,
With all her conscious Majesty confest,
Still bright and brighter wakes th' almighty Flame,   250
To rouse the Feeble and the Wilful tame,
And where she sees the catching Glimpses roll,
Spreads the strong Blaze and all involves the Soul;
But cold Restraints thy conscious Fancy chill,
And formal Passions mock thy struggling Will;
Or, if thy Genius e'er forget his Chain,
And reach impatient at a nobler Strain,
Soon the sad Bodings of contemptuous Mirth
Shoot thro' thy Breast, and stab the generous Birth,
Till, blind with Smart, from Truth to Frenzy tost,   260
And all the Tenour of thy Reason lost,
Perhaps thy Anguish drains a real Tear;
While some with Pity, some with Laughter hear.

*

Tho' bold Corruption boast around the Land,
'Let, Virtue, if she can, my Baits withstand!'   330
Though bolder now she urge th' Accursed claim,
Gay with her Trophies rais'd on CURIO's Shame;

Yet some there are who scorn her impious Mirth,
Who know what Conscience and a Heart are worth.
– O Friend and Father of the human Mind,
Whose Arts for noblest Ends our Frame design'd!
If I, tho' fated to the studious Shade
Which Party-strife, nor anxious Pow'r invade,
If I aspire in public Virtue's Cause
To guide the Muses by sublimer Laws,   340
Do thou her own Authority impart,
And give my Numbers Entrance to the Heart.
Perhaps the Verse might rouze her smother'd Flame,
And snatch the fainting Patriot back to Fame:
Perhaps by worthy Thoughts of human Kind,
To worthy Deeds exalt the conscious Mind;
Or dash Corruption in her proud Career,
And teach her Slaves that Vice was born to fear.

Odes on Several Subjects

X BOOK I:iii   *To a Friend Unsuccessful in Love*

Indeed, my Phaedria, if to find
That wealth can female wishes gain
Had e'er disturbed your thoughtful mind,
Or caused one serious moment's pain,
I should have said that all the rules,
You learn'd of moralists and schools,
Were very useless, very vain.

Yet I perhaps mistake the case –
Say, though with this heroic air,
Like one that holds a nobler chace,   10
You try the tender loss to bear,
Does not your heart renounce your tongue?

Seems not my censure strangely wrong,
To count it such a slight affair?

*

Away with this unmanly mood!
See where the hoary churl appears,   30
Whose hand hath seiz'd the favourite good
Which you reserv'd for happier years:
While, side by side, the blushing maid
Shrinks from his visage, half afraid,
Spite of the sickly joy she wears.

Ye guardian powers of love and fame,
This chaste, harmonious pair behold;
And thus reward the generous flame
Of all who barter vows for gold.
O bloom of youth, o tender charms   40
Well-buried in a dotard's arms!
O equal price of beauty sold!

Cease then to gaze with looks of love:
Bid her adieu, the venal fair:
Unworthy she your bliss to prove;
Then wherefore should she prove your care?
No: lay your myrtle garland down;
And let awhile the willow's crown
With luckier omens bind your hair.

iv   *Affected Indifference. To the Same.*

Yes: you contemn the perjur'd maid
Who all your favourite hopes betray'd:
Nor, though her heart should home return,
Her tuneful tongue its falsehood mourn,
Her winning eyes your faith implore,

51

Would you her hand receive again,
Or once dissemble your disdain,
Or listen to the syren's theme,
Or stoop to love: since now esteem
And confidence, and friendship, is no more.   10

Yet tell me, Phaedria, tell me why,
When summoning your pride you try
To meet her looks with cool neglect,
Or cross her walk with slight respect,
(For so is falsehood best repaid)
Whence do your cheeks indignant glow?
Why is your struggling tongue so slow?
What means that darkness on your brow?
As if with all her broken vow
You meant the fair apostate to upbraid?   20

vi   *Hymn to Cheerfulness*

Is there a youth, whose anxious heart
Labours with love's unpitied smart?
Though now he stray by rills and bowers,   75
And weeping waste the lonely hours,
Or if the nymph her audience deign,
Debase the story of his pain
With slavish looks, discolour'd eyes,
And accents faltering into sighs;
Yet thou, auspicious power, with ease
Canst yield him happier arts to please,
Inform his mien with manlier charms,
Instruct his tongue with nobler arms,
With more commanding passion move,   85
And teach the dignity of love.

Farewell to Leyden's lonely bound,
The Belgian Muse's sober seat;
Where dealing frugal gifts around
To all the favourites at her feet,
She trains the body's bulky frame
For passive, persevering toils;
And lest, from any prouder aim,
The daring mind should scorn her homely spoils,
She breathes maternal fogs to damp its restless flame.

Farewell the grave, pacific air,   10
Where never mountain zephyr blew:
The marshy levels lank and bare,
Which Pan, which Ceres never knew:
The Naiads, with obscene attire,
Urging in vain their urns to flow;
While round them chaunt the croking choir,
And háply soothe some lover's prudent woe,
Or prompt some restive bard and modulate his lyre.

Farewell, ye nymphs, whom, sober love of gain
Snatch'd in your cradles from the god of love: 20
She render'd all his boasted arrows vain;
And all his gifts did he in spite remove.
Ye too, the slow-ey'd fathers of the land,
With whom dominion steals from hand to hand,
Unown'd, undignify'd by public choice,
I go where liberty to all is known,
And tells a monarch on his throne,
He reigns not but by her preserving voice.

O my lov'd England, when with thee
Shall I sit down, to part no more?
Far from this pale, discolor'd sea,   30
That sleeps upon the reedy shore,
When shall I plough thy azure tide?

When on thy hills the flocks admire,
  Like mountain snows; till down their side
I trace the village and the sacred spire,
While bowers and copses green the golden slope divide?

x *To the Muse*

Queen of my songs, harmonious maid,
Ah why hast thou withdrawn thy aid?
Ah why forsaken thus my breast
With inauspicious damps oppress'd?
Where is the dread prophetic heat
With which my bosom wont to beat?
Where all the bright mysterious dreams
Of haunted groves and tuneful streams,
That woo'd my genius to divinest themes?

Say, goddess, can the festal board,   10
Or young Olympia's form ador'd;
Say, can the pomp of promis'd fame
Relume thy faint, thy dying flame?
Or have melodious airs the power
To give one free, poetic hour?
Or, from amid the Elysian train,
The soul of Milton shall I gain,
To win thee back with some celestial strain?

O powerful strain! O sacred soul!
His numbers every sense controul: 20
And now again my bosom burns;
The Muse, the Muse herself returns.
Such on the banks of Tyne, confess'd,
I hail'd the fair immortal guest,
When first she seal'd me for her own,
Made all her blissful treasures known,
And bade me swear to follow her alone.

54

By thought, by dangers, and by toils,
The wreath of just renown is worn;
Nor will ambition's awful spoils   10
The flowery pomp of ease adorn:
But love unbends the force of thought;
By love unmanly fears are taught;
And love's reward with gaudy sloth is bought.

*

So soon again to meet the fair?
So pensive all this absent hour?
– O yet, unlucky youth, beware,
While yet to think is in thy power.
In vain with friendship's flattering name
Thy passion veils its inward shame;
Friendship, the treacherous fuel of thy flame!

Once, I remember, new to love,   50
And dreading his tyrannic chain,
I sought a gentle maid to prove
What peaceful joys in friendship reign:
Whence we forsooth might safely stand,
And pitying view the lovesick band,
And mock the winged boy's malicious hand.

Thus frequent pass'd the cloudless day,
To smiles and sweet discourse resign'd;
While I exulted to survey
One generous woman's real mind: 60
Till friendship soon my languid breast
Each night with unknown cares possess'd,
Dash'd my coy slumbers, or my dreams distress'd.

Fool that I was – And now, even now
While thus I preach the Stoic strain,

Unless I shun Olympia's view,
An hour unsays it all again.
O friend! – when love directs her eyes
To pierce where every passion lies,
Where is the firm, the cautious, or the wise?   70

X xv *To the Evening Star*

To-night retir'd the queen of heaven
    With young Endymion stays:
And now to Hesper is it given
Awhile to rule the vacant sky,
Till she shall to her lamp supply
    A stream of brighter rays.

O Hesper, while the starry throng
    With awe thy path surrounds,
Oh, listen to my suppliant song,
If haply now the vocal sphere   10
Can suffer the delighted ear
    To stoop to mortal sounds.

So may the bridegroom's genial strain
    Thee still invoke to shine:
So may the bride's unmarried train
To Hymen chaunt their flattering vow,
Still that his lucky torch may glow
    With lustre pure as thine.

Far other vows must I prefer
    To thy indulgent power.   20
Alas, but now I paid my tear
On fair Olympia's virgin tomb:
And lo, from thence, in quest I roam
    Of Philomela's bower.

Propitious send thy golden ray,
    Thou purest light above:
Let no false flame seduce to stray
Where gulf or steep lie hid for harm:
But lead where music's healing charm
    May soothe afflicted love.   30

To them, by many a grateful song
    In happier seasons vow'd,
These lawns, Olympia's haunt, belong:
Oft by yon silver stream we walk'd,
Or fix'd, while Philomela talk'd,
    Beneath yon copses stood.

Nor seldom, where the beachen boughs
    That roofless tower invade,
We came while her inchanting Muse
The radiant moon above us held: 40
Till by a clamorous owl compell'd
    She fled the solemn shade.

But hark: I hear her liquid tone.
    Now, Hesper, guide my feet
Down the red marl with moss o'ergrown,
Through yon wild thicket next the plain,
Whose hawthorns choke the winding lane,
    Which leads to her retreat.

See the green space: on either hand
    Enlarg'd it spreads around: 50
See, in the midst she takes her stand,
Where one old oak his awful shade
Extends o'er half the level mead
    Inclos'd in woods profound.

Hark, how through a melting note
   She now prolongs her lays:
How sweetly down the void they float!
The breeze the magic path attends:
The stars shine out: the forest bends:
   The wakeful heifers gaze.   60

Whoe'er thou art whom chance may bring
   To this sequester'd spot,
If then the plaintive Syren sing,
Oh softly tread beneath her bower,
And think of heaven's disposing power,
   Of man's uncertain lot.

Oh think, o'er all this mortal stage,
   What mournful scenes arise:
What ruin waits on kingly rage:
How often virtue dwells with woe: 70
How many griefs from knowledge flow
   How swiftly pleasure flies.

O sacred bird, let me at eve,
   Thus wandering all alone,
Thy tender counsel oft receive,
Bear witness to thy pensive airs,
And pity nature's common cares
   Till I forget my own.

xvi   *To Caleb Hardinge, M.D.*

No, Hardinge: peace to church and state!
That evening, let the Muse give law:
While I anew the theme relate
Which my first youth inamor'd saw.
Then will I oft explore thy thought,
What to reject what Locke hath taught,
What to pursue in Virgil's lay:

Till hope ascends to loftiest things,
Nor envies demagogues or kings
   Their frail and vulgar sway.   50

O vers'd in all the human frame,
Lead thou where'er my labour lies,
And English fancy's eager flame
To Grecian purity chastize:
While hand in hand, at Wisdom's shrine,
Beauty with truth I strive to join,
And grave assent with glad applause;
To paint the story of the soul,
And Plato's visions to control
   By Verulamian laws.   60

BOOK II:i   *The Remonstrance of Shakespeare*

If, yet regardful of your native land,
Old Shakespeare's tongue you deign to understand,
Lo, from the blissful bowers where heaven rewards
Instructive sages and unblemish'd bards,
I come, the ancient founder of this stage,
Intent to learn, in this discerning age,
What form of wit your fancies have imbrac'd,
And whither tends your elegance of taste,
That thus at length our homely toils you spurn,
That thus to foreign scenes you proudly turn,   10
That from my brow the laurel wreath you claim
To crown the rivals of your country's fame.
   What, though the footsteps of my devious Muse
The measur'd walks of Grecian art refuse?
Or though the frankness of my hardy style
Mock the nice touches of the critic's file?
Yet, what my age and climate held to view,
Impartial I survey'd and fearless drew.
And say, ye skillful in the human heart,
Who know to prize a poet's noblest part,   20

What age, what clime, could e'er an ampler field
For lofty thought, for daring fancy, yield?
I saw this England break the shameful bands
Forg'd for the souls of men by sacred hands:
I saw each groaning realm her aid implore;
Her sons the heroes of each warlike shore:
Her naval standard (the dire Spaniard's bane)
Obey'd through all the circuit of the main.
Then too great commerce, for a late-found world,
Around your coast her eager sails unfurl'd: 30
New hopes, new passions, thence the bosom fir'd;
New plans, new arts, the genius thence inspir'd;
Thence every scene, which private fortune knows,
In stronger life, with bolder spirit, rose.

   Disgrac'd I this full prospect which I drew?
My colours languid, or my strokes untrue?
Have not your sages, warriors, swains, and kings,
Confess'd the living draught of men and things?
What other bard in any clime appears
Alike the master of your smiles and tears?   40
Yet have I deign'd your audience to entice
With wretched bribes of luxury and vice?
Or have my various scenes a purpose known
Which freedom, virtue, glory, might not own?

ix   *At Study*

Whither did my fancy stray?
By what magic drawn away
   Have I left my studious theme?
From this philosophic page,
From the problems of the sage,
   Wandering thro' a pleasing dream?

'Tis in vain, alas! I find,
Much in vain, my zealous mind
   Would to learned wisdom's throne

Dedicate each thoughtful hour: 10
Nature bids a softer power
    Claim some minutes for his own.

Let the busy or the wise
View him with contemptuous eyes;
    Love is native to the heart:
Guides its wishes as you will;
Without Love you'll find it still
    Void in one essential part.

Me though no peculiar fair
Touches with a lover's care; 20
    Though the pride of my desire
Asks immortal friendship's name,
Ask the palm of honest fame,
    And the old heroic lyre;

Though the day have smoothly gone,
Or to letter'd leisure known,
    Or in social duty spent;
Yet at eve my lonely breast
Seeks in vain for perfect rest;
    Languishes for true content. 30

xi   *To the Country Gentleman of England*

Whither is Europe's ancient spirit fled?
Where are those valiant tenants of her shore,
Who from the warrior bow the strong dart sped,
Or with firm hand the rapid pole-ax bore?
Freeman and soldier was their common name.
Who late with reapers to the furrow came,
Now in the front of battle charg'd the foe:
Now taught the steer the wintry plough to indure,
Now in full councils check'd incroaching power,
And gave the guardian Laws their majesty to know. 10

But who are ye? from Ebro's loitering sons
To Tiber's pageants, to the sports of Seine;
From Rhine's frail palaces to Danube's thrones
And cities looking on the Cimbric main,
Ye lost, ye self-deserted? whose proud lords
Have baffled your tame hands, and given your swords
To slavish ruffians, hir'd for their command:
These, at some greedy monk's or harlot's nod:
See rifled nations crouch beneath their rod:
These are the public will, the reason of the land.   20

Thou, heedless Albion, what, alas, the while
Dost thou presume? O inexpert in arms,
Yet vain of freedom, how dost thou beguile,
With dreams of hope, these near and loud alarms?
Thy splendid home, thy plan of laws renown'd,
The praise and envy of the nations round,
What care hast thou to guard from fortune's sway?
Amid the storms of war, how soon may all
The lofty pile from its foundations fall,
Of ages the proud toil, the ruin of a day!   30

*

Such were the laurels which your fathers won;
Such glory's dictates in their dauntless breast:
– Is there no voice that speaks to every son?
No nobler, holier call to You address'd?
O! by majestic freedom, righteous laws,
By heavenly truth's, by manly reason's cause,
Awake; attend; be indolent no more:
By friendship, social peace, domestic love,
Rise; arm; your country's living safety prove;
And train her valiant youth, and watch around her shore.   160

Away! away!
Tempt me no more, insidious love:
    Thy soothing sway
Long did my youthful bosom prove:
At length thy treason is discern'd,
At length some dear-bought caution earn'd:
Away! nor hope my riper age to move.

I know, I see
Her merit. Needs it now be shewn,
    Alas, to me?   10
How often, to myself unknown,
The graceful, gentle, virtuous maid
Have I admir'd! How often said,
What joy to call a heart like hers one's own!

But, flattering god,
O squanderer of content and ease,
    In thy abode
Will care's rude lesson learn to please?
O say, deceiver, hast thou won
Proud fortune to attend thy throne,   20
Or plac'd thy friends above her stern decrees?

Hymn to the Naiads

Hail, ye who share the stern Minerva's power;
Who arm the hand of Liberty for war:
And give to the renown'd Britannic name
To awe contending monarchs: yet benign,
Yet mild of nature: to the works of peace
More prone, and lenient of the many ills   170
Which wait on human life. Your gentle aid

63

Hygeia well can witness; she who saves,
From poisonous cates and cups of pleasing bane,
The wretch devoted to the entangling snares
Of Bacchus and of Comus. Him she leads
To Cynthia's lonely haunts. To spread the toils,
To beat the coverts, with the jovial horn
At dawn of day to summon the loud hounds,
She calls the lingering sluggard from his dreams:
And where his breast may drink the mountain breeze,   180
And where the fervour of the sunny vale
May beat upon his brow, through devious paths
Beckons his rapid courser. Nor when ease,
Cool ease and welcome slumbers have becalm'd
His eager bosom, does the queen of health
Her pleasing care withhold. His decent board
She guards, presiding; and the frugal powers
With joy sedate leads in: and while the brown
Ennaean dame with Pan presents her stores;
While changing still, and comely in the change,   190
Vertumnus and the Hours before him spread
The garden's banquet, you to crown his feast,
To crown his feast, O Naiads, you the fair
Hygeia calls: and from your shelving seats,
And groves of poplar, plenteous cups ye bring,
To slake his veins: till soon a purer tide
Flows down those loaded channels; washeth off
The dregs of luxury, the lurking seeds
Of crude disease; and through the abodes of life
Sends vigour, sends repose. Hail, Naiads: hail,   200
Who give, to labour, health; to stooping age,
The joys which youth hath squander'd. Oft your urns
Will I invoke; and frequent in your praise,
Abash the frantic Thyrsus with my song.

Inscriptions

I *For a Grotto*
To me, whom in their lays the shepherds call
Actaea, daughter of the neighbouring stream,
This cave, belongs. The fig-tree and the vine,
Which o'er the rocky entrance downward shoot,
Were plac'd by Glycon. He with cowslips pale,
Primrose, and purple lychnis, deck'd the green
Before my threshold, and my shelving walls
With honeysuckle cover'd. Here at noon,
Lull'd by the murmur of my rising fount,
I slumber: here my clustering fruits I tend: 10
Or from the humid flowers, at break of day,
Fresh garlands weave, and chace from all my bounds
Each thing impure or noxious. Enter in,
O stranger, undismay'd. Nor bat, nor toad
Here lurks: and if thy breast of blameless thoughts
Approve thee, not unwelcome shalt thou tread
My quiet mansion: chiefly if thy name
Wise Pallas and the immortal Muses own.

II *For a Statue of Chaucer at Woodstock*
Such was old Chaucer. such the placid mien
Of him who first with harmony inform'd
The language of our fathers. Here he dwelt
For many a cheerful day. These ancient walls
Have often heard him, while his legends blithe
He sang; of love, or knighthood, or the wiles
Of homely life: through each estate and age,
The fashions and the follies of the world
With cunning hand portraying. Though perchance
From Blenheim's towers, o stranger thou art come   10
Glowing with Churchill's trophies; yet in vain
Dost thou applaud them if thy breast be cold
To him, this other hero; who in times

65

Dark and untaught, began with charming verse
To tame the rudeness of his native land.

IV

O youths and virgins: o declining eld:
O pale misfortune's slaves: o ye who dwell
Unknown with humble quiet; ye who wait
In courts, or fill the golden seat of kings:
O sons of sport and pleasure: o thou wretch
That weep'st for jealous love, or the sore wounds
Of conscious guilt, or death's rapacious hand
Which left thee void of hope: o ye who roam
In exile; ye who through the embattled field
Seek bright renown; or who for nobler palms   10
Contend, the leaders of a public cause;
Approach: behold this marble. Know ye not
The features? Hath not oft his faithful tongue
Told you the fashion of your own estate,
The secrets of your bosom? Here then, round
His monument with reverence while ye stand,
Say to each other: 'This was Shakespeare's form;
Who walk'd in every path of human life,
Felt every passion; and to all mankind
Doth now, will ever, that experience yield   20
Which his own genius only could acquire.'

VI

Thou, who the verdant plain dost traverse here,
While Thames among his willows from thy view
Retires; o stranger, stay thee, and the scene
Around contemplate well. This is the place
Where England's ancient barons, clad in arms
And stern with conquest, from their tyrant king
(Then render'd tame) did challenge and secure
The charter of thy freedom. Pass not on

Till thou hast bless'd their memory, and paid
Those thanks which God appointed the reward   10
Of public virtue. and if chance thy home
Salute thee with a father's honour'd name,
Go, call thy sons: instruct them what a debt
They owe their ancestors; and make them swear
To pay it, by transmitting down intire
Those sacred rights to which themselves were born.

VIII
Ye powers unseen, to whom, the bards of Greece
Erected altars; ye who to the mind
More lofty views unfold, and prompt the heart
With more divine emotions; if ere while
Not quite unpleasing have my votive rites
Of you been deem'd, when oft this lonely seat
To you I consecrated; then vouchsafe
Here with your instant energy to crown
My happy solitude. It is the hour
When most I love to invoke you, and have felt   10
Most frequent your glad ministry divine.
The air is calm: the sun's unveiled orb
Shines in the middle heaven. the harvest round
Stands quiet, and among the golden sheaves
The reapers lie reclin'd. The neighbouring groves
Are mute; nor even a linnet's random strain
Echoeth amid the silence. Let me feel
Your influence, ye kind powers. Aloft in heaven,
Abide ye? or on those transparent clouds
Pass ye from hill to hill? or on the shades   20
Which yonder elms cast o'er the lake below
Do you converse retir'd? From what lov'd haunt
Shall I expect you? Let me once more feel
Your influence, o ye kind inspiring powers:
And I will guard it well, nor shall a thought
Rise in my mind, nor shall a passion move

Across my bosom unobserv'd, unstor'd
By faithful memory. and then at some
More active moment, will I call them forth
Anew; and join them in majestic forms,   30
And give them utterances in harmonious strains;
That all mankind shall wonder at your sway.

The Pleasures of the Imagination
(revised version)

I

With what inchantment Nature's goodly scene
Attracts the sense of mortals; how the mind
For its own eye doth objects nobler still
Prepare; how men by various lessons learn
To judge of beauty's praise; what raptures fill
The breast with fancy's native arts indowed,
And what true culture guides it to renown;
My verse unfolds. Ye gods, or godlike powers,
Ye guardians of the sacred task, attend
Propitious. Hand in hand around your bard   10
Move in majestic measures, leading on
His doubtful step thro' many a solemn path,
Conscious of secrets which to human sight
Ye only can reveal. Be great in him:
And let your favour make him wise to speak
Of all your wondrous empire; with a voice
So temper'd to his theme, that those, who hear,
May yield perpetual homage to yourselves.
Thou chief, O daughter of eternal Love,
Whate'er thy name; or Muse, or Grace, ador'd   20
By Grecian prophets; to the sons of Heaven
Known, while with deep amazement thou dost there
The perfect counsels read, the ideas old,

Of thine omniscient Father; known on earth
By the still horror and the blissful tear
With which thou seizest on the soul of man;
Thou chief, Poetic Spirit, from the banks
Of Avon, whence thy holy fingers cull
Fresh flowers and dews to sprinkle on the turf
Where Shakespeare lies, be present. And with thee   30
Let Fiction come; on her aeriel wings
Wafting ten thousand colours; which in sport,
By the light glances of her magic eye,
She blends and shifts at will thro' countless forms,
Her wild creation. Goddess of the lyre,
Whose awful tones controul the moving sphere,
Wilt thou, eternal Harmony, descend,
And join this happy train? for with thee comes
The guide, the guardian of their mystic rites,
Wise Order: and, where Order deigns to come,   40
Her sister, Liberty, will not be far.
Be present all ye Genii, who conduct
Of youthful bards the lonely-wandering step
New to your springs and shades; who touch their ear
With finer sounds, and heighten to their eye
The pomp of nature, and before them place
The fairest, loftiest countenance of things.

II
But from what name, what favourite sign,
What heavenly auspice, rather shall I date
My perilous excursion, than from truth,
That nearest inmate of the human soul;
Estrang'd from whom the countenance divine
Of man disfigur'd and dishonour'd sinks
Among inferior things? For to the brutes
Perception and the transient boons of sense
Hath fate imparted: but to man alone   50

69

Of sublunary beings was it given
Each fleeting impulse on the sensual powers
At leisure to review; with equal eye
To scan the passion of the stricken nerve,
Or the vague object striking: to conduct
From sense, the portal turbulent and loud,
Into the mind's wide palace one by one
The frequent, pressing, fluctuating forms,
And question and compare them. Thus he learns
Their birth and fortunes; how allied they haunt   60
The avenues of sense; what laws direct
Their union; and what various discords rise,
Or fixed or casual: which when his clear thought
Retains and when his faithful words express,
That living image of the external scene,
As in a polish'd mirror held to view,
Is truth: whate'er it varies from the shape
And hue of its exemplar, in that part
Dim error lurks.

*

    Hitherto the stores,
Which feed thy mind and exercise her powers,
Partake the relish of their native soil,   100
Their parent earth. But know, a nobler dower
Her sire at birth decreed her; purer gifts
From his own treasure; forms which never deign'd
In eyes or ears to dwell, within the sense
Of earthly organs; but sublime were plac'd
In his essential reason, leading there
That vast ideal host which all his works
Thro' endless ages never will reveal.
Thus then indow'd, the feeble creature man,
The slave of hunger and the prey of death,   110
Even now, even here, in earth's dim prison bound,

The language of intelligence divine
Attains...

*

    Such the rise of forms
Sequester'd far from sense and every spot
Peculiar in the realms of space or time:
Such is the throne which man from truth amid
The paths of mutability hath built
Secure, unshaken, still; and whence he views
In matter's mouldering structures, the pure forms
Of triangle or circle, cube or cone,
Impassive all; whose attributes nor force
Nor fate can alter. There he first conceives   140
True being, and an intellectual world
The same this hour and ever. Thence he deems
Of his own lot; above the painted shapes
That fleeting move o'er this terrestrial scene
Looks up; beyond the adamantine gates
Of death expatiates; as his birthright claims
Inheritance in all the works of God;
Prepares for endless time his plan of life,
And counts the universe itself his home.

IV
A different task remains; the secret paths   20
Of early genius to explore: to trace
Those haunts where Fancy her predestin'd sons,
Like to the Demigods of old, doth nurse
Remote from eyes profane. Ye happy souls
Who now her tender discipline obey,
Where dwell ye? What wild river's brink at eve
Imprint your steps? What solemn groves at noon
Use ye to visit, often breaking forth
In rapture 'mid your dilatory walk,

Or musing, as in slumber, on the green?   30
– Would I again were you! – O ye dales
Of Tyne, and ye most ancient woodlands; where
Oft as the giant flood obliquely strides,
And his banks open, and his lawns extend,
Stops short the pleased traveller to view
Presiding o'er the scene some rustic tower
Founded by Norman or by Saxon hands:
O ye Northumbrian shades, which overlook
The rocky pavement and the mossy falls
Of solitary Wensbeck's limpid stream;   40
How gladly I recall your well-known seats
Belov'd of old, and that delightful time
When all alone, for many a summer's day,
I wander'd thro' your calm recesses, led
In silence by some powerful hand unseen.

    Nor will I e'er forget you, nor shall e'er
The graver tasks of manhood, or the advice
Of vulgar wisdom, move me to disclaim
Those studies which possessed me in the dawn
Of life, and fix'd the color of my mind   50
For every future year: whence even now
From sleep I rescue the clear hours of morn,
And, while the world around lies overwhelm'd
In idle darkness, am alive to thoughts
Of honourable fame, of truth divine
Or moral, and of minds to virtue won
By the sweet magic of harmonious verse;
The themes which now expect us. For thus far
On general habits, and on arts which grow
Spontaneous in the minds of all mankind   60
Hath dwelt our argument; and how self-taught,
Though seldom conscious of their own imploy,
In nature's or in fortune's changeful scene
Men learn to judge of beauty, and acquire
Those forms set up, as idols in the soul
For love and zealous praise. Yet indistinct,

In vulgar bosoms, and unnotic'd lie
These pleasing stores, unless the casual force
Of things external prompt the heedless mind
To recognize her wealth. But some there are   70
Conscious of nature, and the rule which man
O'er Nature holds: some who, within themselves
Retiring from the trivial scenes of chance
And momentary passion, can at will
Call up these fair exemplars of the mind;
Review their features; scan the secret laws
Which bind them to each other: and display
By forms, or sounds, or colours, to the sense
Of all the world their latent charms display:
Even as in nature's frame (if such a word,   80
If such a word, so bold, may from the lips
Of man proceed) as in this outward frame
Of things, the great Artificer portrays
His own immense idea.

*

                              . . . the chief
Are poets; eloquent men, who dwell on earth
To clothe whate'er the soul admires or loves
With language and with numbers. Hence to these
A field is open'd wide as nature's sphere;
Nay, wider: various as the sudden acts
Of human wit, and vast as the demands
Of human will. The bard nor length, nor depth,
Nor place, nor form controuls. To eyes, to ears,
To every organ of the copious mind,   110
He offereth all his treasures. Him the hours,
The seasons him obey: and changeful Time
Sees him at will keep measure with his flight,
At will outstrip it. To enhance his toil,
He summoneth from the uttermost extent
Of things which God hath taught him, every form

73

Auxiliar, every power; and all beside
Excludes imperious. His prevailing hand
Gives, to corporeal essence, life and sense
And every stately function of the soul.   120
The soul itself to him obsequious lies,
Like matter's passive heap; and as he wills
To reason and affection he assigns
Their just alliances, their just degrees:
Whence his peculiar honours: whence the race
Of men who people his delightful world,
Men genuine and according to themselves,
Transcend as far the uncertain sons of earth,
As earth itself to his delightful world
The palm of spotless Beauty doth resign.   130

James Macpherson

'Sir, a man might write such stuff for ever, if he would abandon his mind to it'. James Macpherson, the 'translator' of Ossian, son of Fingal and bard to the ancient Caledonians, had little choice but to demand a retraction after Johnson's brusque dismissal. Predictably enough, this was unforth-coming and subsequent threats of duels and other forms of physical retribution received the imperious response: 'What would you have me retract? I thought your book an imposture; I think it an imposture still. For this opinion I have given my reasons to the publick, which I here dare you to refute'.[1]

Johnson's 'reasons' amounted to little more than a general prejudice against Scottish culture and the mistaken assumption that no manuscripts could exist in a language such as Gaelic that had only recently been trans-cribed. Yet on the whole his verdict has been regarded as conclusive: the triumph of robust good sense against bullying charlatanism. There has been scant sympathy for the twenty-two-year-old itinerant Scottish school-master, whose forgeries, having beguiled the Edinburgh intelligentsia, provided the basis for a substantial political career in London, and an even-tual return home as laird of his valley. His success has been held against him; and when we find Blake declaring himself 'an admirer of Ossian equally with any other poet whatsoever', or Hazlitt placing his writings along 'the four principal pieces of poetry in the world', we are likely to wonder, with Swinburne, 'how or why such lank and lamentable counter-feits of the poetical style ever gained this luckless influence'.[2]

Macpherson was born at Ruthven near Inverness in 1736, a farmer's son, and experienced at first hand the second Jacobite rebellion in 1745. (It is possible that he witnessed the bloody aftermath of Culloden as Cumber-land's troops pursued the routed army through his home valley.) Certainly one should never forget the political dimension of Ossian's laments for a lost king, and his idealization of the warrior-clans that were being sys-tematically destroyed in the great clearances. (The Jacobite sympathies can be clearly seen in *The Hunter*'s celebration of patriotic struggle against the Saxon foe.) But it is wrong to regard Macpherson as some kind of wild boy from the mountains. He studied classics at the prestigious Marischal Col-lege in Aberdeen between 1752 and 1755,[3] composed his primitivist epics on strict Aristotelian principles, and went on to publish a respectable prose version of *The Iliad*.

By the late 1750s he had become sufficiently interested in Gaelic to have acquired a collection of manuscripts. While teaching at Moffat in 1759, he was asked by John Home to produce some translations: he chose to substi-tute his own composition, 'The Death of Oscar'. This was enthusiastically received and rapidly followed by others; of the fifteen pieces published in *Fragments of Ancient Poetry* in 1760, only two are based on extant originals.

75

The main ingredients of the Ossianic style are already present: expiring heroes, picturesque wilderness, elliptical narrative, plangent septenaries, all delivered in a continuous elegiac monologue, for which Macpherson coined the phrase 'joy of grief'. His 1773 preface acknowledges, with delicately explicit irony: 'the following Poems, it must be confessed, are... calculated to please persons of exquisite feelings of heart'. It should be stressed that their initial audience was not some sentimentalist mass-market but composed of sophisticated intellectuals. Macpherson had shrewdly hinted at the possibility of finding an entire epic, and the subsequent contributors read like a roll-call of the Scottish Enlightenment: Hugh Blair, Adam Fergusson, David Hume, James Beattie, William Robertson.

It appears that the quest was to some extent sincerely undertaken. Macpherson travelled to Skye, where the minister, John Macpherson, remembered Ossianic poems recited by wandering bards; and to Benbecula, where MacDonald of Clanranald still kept a hereditary bard and possessed numerous manuscripts. (These, which Macpherson borrowed without ever returning, were the documentary evidence which he would later offer in his own defence.) He emerged a few months later with the draft of *Fingal, an Ancient Epic Poem* to receive a euphoric welcome as the retriever of a genuine Scottish epic. It is not necessary to appeal to some mystical racial essence, what Matthew Arnold termed the 'very soul of the Celtic genius',[4] to comprehend the political attractiveness of Ossian as the founding myth of an independent national culture. (There was no pressure to provide documentary evidence at this stage, despite the ready availability of Gaelic experts.) An introduction was procured from Lord Bute, then prime minister, who funded the publication of *Fingal* in 1762. Macpherson pushed his luck rather too hard by putting out a second long poem, *Temora*, in 1763. Opinion in London, initially wavering, swung sharply against him: despite Macpherson's obstinate refusal to provide further proof, Edinburgh, with the single exception of Hume, stayed solidly loyal.

Macpherson detached himself from the fray, allowing his supporters to conduct his defence for him. His interest had shifted to politics: after two years as secretary to the governor of Florida, he landed the lucrative position of London agent for the Nawab of Arcot, for which he received 12,000 pagodas plus expenses plus, of course, bribes. He claimed to have become the real ruler of India, responsible for the unseating of Warren Hastings and the insertion of a whole nest of Macphersons into the interim administration. (One of the nicer ironies of the affair is the severe embarrassment which the grateful Highlanders caused their benefactor when in the 1790s they publicly offered to finance the printing of the original manuscripts of Ossian in order to clear his name.) Throughout the 1770s Macpherson produced a series of historical works supporting the Hanoverian dynasty, for which he was paid £3000. He also received a pension of £600 for producing a series of pamphlets on the victorious progress of the American war (otherwise known as 'Macpherson's daily column of lies'): exactly twice as much as that other notable literary pensioner of the North Administration, Samuel Johnson. He entered Parliament in 1780, became an effective lobbyist (without ever bothering to deliver a speech), and eventually retired to the estate of Belleville in Inverness, to a house built by Robert Adam, with the chief of his clan as tame house-guest. When he died in 1796, he was buried in Westminster Abbey (admittedly at his own expense, but the gesture is indicative of his progressively less veiled regard for his own poetic talent). If as Johnson claimed, 'no man but a blockhead ever wrote, except for money',[5] then Macpherson must rank alongside Pope as success story of the century – and in terms of European reputation, far outstripped him. Goethe's Werther spends his last night with Charlotte reciting *The Songs of Selma*; Napoleon read the poems on the homeward voyage from Egypt and the outward journey to St Helena; his marshal, Bernadotte, made emperor of Sweden, would ensure the continuation of his dynasty by calling his heir Oscar, after the son of Ossian.

To return to Johnson's initial comment: in what sense is the mind 'abandoned' in Ossian? Most obviously, there is a near-total absence of grammatical complexity and abstract vocabulary; Ossian's landscapes are composed through an extreme form of *pointillisme*, a style entirely dependent on the discrete notation of particulars, whose rapidity and disconnection almost enact the continuous patter of sense-data on the retina. It is, as the original preface to the 'Fragments' claims, 'extremely literal'. Hence the irony of Wordsworth's famous denunciation of the 'thin Consistence' of Ossianic rhetoric: his own primitivist argument that 'elementary feelings' are revealed in rural communities because of 'the sameness and narrow circle of their intercourse'[6] is prefigured by Macpherson's practice of concentration through limitation.

Hazlitt eloquently brings out the implications of this psychology:

> Ossian... is a feeling and a name that can never be destroyed in the minds of his readers. As Homer is the first vigour and lustihead, Ossian is the decay and old age of poetry. He lives only in the recollection and regret of the past. There is one impression that he conveys more entirely than all other poets, namely the sense of privation, the loss of all things, of friends, of good name, of country – he is even without God in the world. He converses only with spirits of the departed; with the motionless and silent clouds... The feeling of cheerless desolation, of the loss of the pith and the sap of existence, of the annihilation of the substance, and the clinging to the shadow of all things as in a mock embrace is here perfect...[7]

Ossian, 'a feeling and a name', exists 'only in recollection and regret of the past': we peer into him, through him, to a landscape suffused with 'decay and old age'. Hazlitt makes no attempt to mitigate the 'cheerless desolation', even by invoking 'joy of grief', but instead finds a logical satisfaction in its 'perfect' completeness. Behind this concept of memory as imprisonment and decay into eventual and utter oblivion lies Locke's sombre account of 'Retention': 'Thus the *Ideas*, as well as Children of our Youth, often die before us: And our Minds represent to us those Tombs, to which we are approaching' (2:10:5).

In Macpherson, the 'ground-work' of the narrator – solitary, verging on death, totally removed from the replenishment of a human or even sensory present – becomes more important than what is related. Ossian's only mental activity is remembering: seizing the 'shadowy thoughts that fly across my soul'; re-etching memories onto the 'failing soul'; preparing for the moment when all must be laid in the 'dark house' of the psyche. The ageing mind is a 'cave of streams', a rigidly immobile container whose finite 'stock' of memories is constantly washed away. Change is momentarily arrested, held at bay, for the duration of the telling, which, however, dwells obsessively on the treacherous motion of the 'dark-brown years'.

The ghosts which haunt the Ossianic landscape must be understood in the context of this spectrality of retrospect. Rather than representing violent incursions from supernatural worlds, these spirits are mundane, even pitiful: the 'spirit of Loda' is easily defeated. In the most extended account of the after-life, in *Berrathon*, things have no solidity, are half-dissolved back into cloud and mist; Malvina's 'blush' appears incongruously physical. The spirits are best regarded as an intermediate stage between the living participants and the landscape itself, subject to the constant threat of dispersal and extinction. Their continued survival depends on being recharged by entirely secular acts of remembrance. One can be dying before death, in the decline of one's personal memories and public reputation: paradoxically, one can continue dying after it. Hence the overriding imperative to achieve, conserve and accumulate fame: no actual warfare seems to happen on the battlefield, only an intricate system of recognition and exchange of compliment.[8] A similar structure is apparent in the dialogue between Shilric and Vinvela and elsewhere: love in Macpherson is motivated by a commitment to preserve a future memory, the most intimate of all human bonds.

I have tried in these selections to bring out the structural coherence of the Ossianic milieu: the way the stance of elegiac retrospect is supported through the ethic of fame, the ancestral burden, the spirits, the autumnal landscapes, and the pervasive imagery of decay. To this end, I have chosen to group the extracts thematically, with only *Oi-thona* and *The Songs of Selma* given in their entirety, in preference to following the overall narrative ordering (vestigial to the point of invisibility) or chronology of composition (all the texts are written within a four-year period, 1759-63). The pieces taken from Macpherson's other poetry are intended to allow an assess-

78

ment of how much (or how little) he gains from the use of the Ossianic persona.

The impact of Ossian on primitivism, the gothic, and the picturesque has an undoubted historical importance. But can the present-day reader find anything other than what Johnson called 'a mere unconnected rhapsody, a tiresome repetition of the same images'9? What becomes increasingly impressive is the way Macpherson remains within the closed system, refuses to lay claim to a personal transcendence. I would single out the final codas. Here the narrative present both addresses itself to an unspecified future audience and holds itself back in a past as far off as the period which it itself laments. There is a fusion of the agony of immediate personal loss with a sense of cultural transience requiring a distant retrospect. But without defeatism: the keeping of faith through commemoration becomes the only durable tie in the face of a common oblivion. Thus Macpherson remains, I think, a humanist, and as representative an Augustan voice as Johnson: his text displays a stoicism in the face of personal mortality and a cultural solidarity, a respect for enclaves of human community amidst a bleak expanse of secular time.

Fragments of Ancient Poetry Collected in the Highlands of Scotland and Translated from the Galic or Erse Language

PREFACE

The public may depend on the following fragments as genuine remains of ancient Scottish poetry. The date of their composition cannot be exactly ascertained. Tradition, in the country where they were written, refers them to an aera of the most remote antiquity: and this tradition is supported by the spirit and strain of the poems themselves; which abound with those ideas, and paint those manners, that belong to the most early state of society. The diction too, in the original, is very obsolete; and differs widely from the style of such poems as have been written in the same language two or three centuries ago. They were certainly composed before the establishment of clanship in the northern part of Scotland, which is itself very ancient; for had clans been then formed and known, they must have made a considerable

79

figure in the work of a Highland Bard; whereas there is not the least mention of them in these poems. It is remarkable that there are found no allusions to the Christian religion or worship; indeed, few traces of religion of any kind...

Though the poems now published appear as detached pieces in this collection, there is ground to believe that most of them were originally episodes of a greater work which related to the wars of Fingal. Concerning this hero innumerable traditions remain, to this day, in the Highlands of Scotland. The story of Oscian, his son, is so generally known, that to describe one in whom the race of a great family ends, it has passed into a proverb: 'Oscian the "last of the heroes"'.

There can be no doubt that these poems are to be ascribed to the Bards; a race of men well known to have continued throughout many ages in Ireland and the north of Scotland. Every chief or great man had in his family a Bard or poet, whose office it was to record in verse, the illustrious actions of that family. By the succession of these Bards, such poems were handed down from race to race; some in manuscript, but more by oral tradition. And tradition, in a country so free of intermixture with foreigners, and among a people so strongly attached to the memory of their ancestors, has preserved many of them in a great measure incorrupted to this day.

They are not set to music, nor sung. The versification in the original is simple; and to such as understand the language, very smooth and beautiful. Rhyme is seldom used: but the cadence, and the length of the line varied, so as to suit the sense. The translation is extremely literal. Even the arrangement of the words in the original has been imitated; to which must be imputed some inversions in the style, that otherwise would not have been chosen.

Of the poetical merit of these fragments nothing shall here be said. Let the public judge, and pronounce. It is believed, that, by a careful inquiry, many more remains of ancient genius, no less valuable than those now given to the world, might be found in the same country where these have been collected. In particular there is reason to hope that one work of considerable length, and which deserves to be styled an heroic poem, might be recovered and translated, if encouragement were given to such an undertaking... The three last poems in the collection are fragments which the translator obtained of this Epic poem; and tho' very imperfect, they were judged not unworthy of being inserted. If the whole were recovered it might serve to throw considerable light upon the Scottish and Irish antiquities.

I   SHILRIC, VINVELA

Vinvela.

My love is a son of the hill. He pursues the flying deer. His gray dogs are panting around him; his bow-string sounds in the wind. Whether by the fount of the rock or by the stream of the mountain thou liest; when the rushes are nodding with the wind, and the mist is flying over thee, let me approach my love unperceived, and see him from the rock. Lovely I saw thee first by the aged oak of Branno; thou wert returning tall from the chace; the fairest among thy friends.

Shilric.

What voice is it that I hear? that voice like the summer-wind. I sit not by the nodding rushes; I hear not the fount of the rock. Afar, Vinvela, afar I go to the wars of Fingal. My dogs attend me no more. No more I tread the hill. No more from on high I see thee, fair-moving by the stream of the plain; bright as the bow of heaven; as the moon on the western wave.

Vinvela.

Then thou art gone, O Shilric! and I am alone on the hill. The deer are seen on the brow; void of fear they graze along. No more they dread the wind; no more the rustling tree. The hunter is far removed; he is in the field of graves. Strangers! sons of the waves! spare my lovely Shilric!

Shilric.

If fall I must in the field, raise high my grave, Vinvela. Grey

81

stones, and heaped-up earth, shall mark me to future times. When the hunter shall sit by the mound, and produce his food at noon, 'Some warrior rests here,' he will say; and my fame shall live in his praise. Remember me, Vinvela, when low on earth I lie!

Vinvela.

Yes! – I will remember thee – indeed my Shilric will fall. What shall I do, my love! when thou art gone for ever? Through these hills I will go at noon: I will go through the silent heath. There I will see the place of thy rest, returning from the chace. Indeed, my Shilric will fall; but I will remember him.

II

I sit by the mossy fountain; on the top of the hill of winds. One tree is rustling above me. Dark waves roll over the heath. The lake is troubled below. The deer descend from the hill. No hunter at a distance is seen; no whistling cow-herd is nigh. It is mid-day: but all is silent. Sad are my thoughts alone. Didst thou but appear, O my love, a wanderer on the heath! thy hair floating on the wind behind thee; thy bosom heaving on the sight; thine eyes full of fears for thy friends, whom the mist of the hill had concealed! Thee I would comfort, my love, and bring thee to thy father's house.

But is it she that there appears, like a beam of light on the heath? bright as the moon in autumn, as the sun in a summer-storm, comest thou lovely maid, over rocks, over mountains to me? – She speaks: but how weak her voice! like the breeze in the reeds of the pool. Hark!

Returnest thou safe from the war? Where are thy friends, my love? I heard of thy death on the hill; I heard and mourned thee, Shilric!

Yes, my fair, I return; but I alone of my race. Thou shalt see them no more: their graves I raised on the plain. But why art thou on the desert hill? why on the heath, alone?

Alone I am, O Shilric! alone in the winter-house. With grief for thee I expired. Shilric, I am pale in the tomb.

She fleets, she sails away; as grey mist before the wind! – and, wilt thou not stay, my love? Stay and behold my tears! fair thou appearest, my love! fair thou wast, when alive!

By the mossy fountain I will sit; on the top of the hill of winds. When mid-day is silent around, converse, O my love, with me! come on the wings of the gale! on the blast of the mountain, come! Let me hear thy voice, as thou passest, when mid-day is silent around.

V

Autumn is dark on the mountains; grey mist rests on the hills. The whirlwind is heard on the heath. Dark rolls the river thro' the narrow plain. A tree stands alone on the hill, and marks the grave of Connal. The leaves whirl round with the wind, and strew the grave of the dead. At times are seen here the ghosts of the deceased, when the musing hunter alone stalks slowly over the heath. Appear in thy armour of light, thou ghost of mighty Connal! Shine, near thy tomb, Crimora! like a moon-beam from a cloud.

Who can search the source of thy race, O Connal? and who recount thy Fathers? Thy family grew like an oak on the mountains, which meeteth the wind with its lofty head. But now it is torn from the earth. Who shall supply the place of Connal?

Here was the din of arms; and here the groans of the dying. Mournful are the wars of Fingal! O Connal! it was here thou didst fall. Thine arm was like a storm; thy sword, a beam of the sky; thy height, a rock on the plain; thine eyes, a furnace of fire. Louder than a storm was thy voice, when thou confoundest the field. Warriors fell by thy sword, as the thistle by the staff of a boy.

Dargo the mighty came on, like a cloud of thunder. His brows were contracted and dark. His eyes like two caves in a rock. Bright rose their swords on each side; dire was the clang of their steel.

The daughter of Rinval was near; Crimora, bright in the armour of man; her hair loose behind, her bow in her hand. She followed the youth to the war, Connal her much-beloved. She drew the string on Dargo; but erring pierced her Connal. He falls like an oak on the plain; like a rock from the shaggy hill. What shall she do, hapless maid! He bleeds; her Connal dies. All the night long she cries, and all the day, O Connal, my love and my friend! With grief the sad mourner died.

Earth here incloseth the loveliest pair on the hill. The grass grows between the stones of their tomb; I sit in the mournful shade. The wind sighs through the grass; and their memory rushes on my mind. Undisturbed you now sleep together; in the tomb of the mountain you rest alone.

VI

Son of the noble Fingal, Oscian, prince of men! what tears run down the cheeks of age? what shades thy mighty soul?

Memory, son of Alpin, memory wounds the aged. Of former times are my thoughts; my thoughts are of the noble Fingal. The race of the king return into my mind, and wound me with remembrance.

One day, returned from the sport of the mountains, from pursuing the sons of the hill, we covered this heath with our youth. Fingal the mighty was here, and Oscur, my son, great in war. Fair on our sight from the sea, at once, a virgin came. Her breast was like the snow of one night. Her cheek like the bud of the rose. Mild was her blue-rolling eye: but sorrow was big in her heart.

Fingal renowned in war! she cries, sons of the king, preserve me! Speak secure, replies the king, daughter of beauty, speak: our ear is open to all: our swords redress the injured. I fly from Ullin, she cries; from Ullin, famous in war. I fly from the embrace of him who would debase my blood. Cremor! the friend of men, was my father; Cremor the prince of Inverne.

Fingal's younger sons arose; Carryl expert in the bow; Fillan beloved of the fair; and Fergus first in the race. – Who from the farthest Lochlyn? who to the seas of Molochasquir? who dares hurt the maid whom the sons of Fingal guard? Daughter of beauty, rest secure; rest in peace, thou fairest of women.

Far in the blue distance of the deep, some spot appeared like the back of the ridge-wave. But soon the ship increased on our sight. The hand of Ullin drew her to land. The mountains trembled as he moved. The hills shook at his step. Dire rattled his armour around him. Death and destruction were in his eyes. His stature like the oak of Morven. He moved in the lightning of steel.

Our warriors fell before him, like the field before the reapers. Fingal's three sons he bound. He plunged his sword into the fair one's breast. She fell as a wreath of snow before the sun in spring. Her bosom heaved in death; her soul came forth in blood.

Oscur my son came down; the mighty in battle descended. His armour rattled in thunder; and the lightning of his eyes was terrible. There, was the clashing of swords; there, was the voice of steel. They struck and they thrust; they digged for death with their swords. But death was distant far, and delayed to come. The sun began to decline; and the cow-herd thought of home. Then Oscur's keen steel found the heart of Ullin. He fell like a mountain-oak covered over with glistering frost: He shone like a rock on the plain. – Here the daughter of beauty lieth; and here the bravest of men. Here one day ended the fair and the valiant. Here rest the pursuer and the pursued.

Son of Alpin! the woes of the aged are many: their tears are for the past. This raised my sorrow, warrior; memory awaked my grief. Oscur my son was brave; but Oscur is now no more. Thou hast my grief, O son of Alpin; forgive the tears of the aged.

VIII

By the side of a rock on the hill, beneath the aged trees, old Oscian sat on the moss; the last of the race of Fingal. Sightless are his aged eyes; his beard is waving in the wind. Dull through the leafless trees he heard the voice of the north. Sorrow revived in his soul: he began and lamented the dead.

How hast thou fallen like an oak, with all thy branches round thee! Where is Fingal the King? where is Oscur my son? where are all my race? Alas! in the earth they lie. I feel their tombs with my hands. I hear the river below murmuring hoarsely over the stones. What dost thou, O river, to me? Thou bringest back the memory of the past.

The race of Fingal stood on thy banks, like a wood in a fertile soil. Keen were their spears of steel. Hardy was he who dared to encounter their rage. Fillan the great was there. Thou Oscur wert there, my son! Fingal himself was there, strong in the grey locks of years. Full rose his sinewy limbs; and wide his shoulders spread. The unhappy met his arm, when the pride of his wrath arose.

The son of Morny came; Gaul, the tallest of men. He stood on the hill like an oak! His voice was like the streams of the hill. Why reigneth alone, he cries, the son of mighty Corval? Fingal is not strong to save: he is no support for the people. I am strong as a storm in the ocean; as a whirlwind on the hill. Yield, son of Corval; Fingal, yield to me. He came like a rock from the hill, resounding in his arms.

Oscur stood forth to meet him; my son would meet the foe. But Fingal came in his strength, and smiled at the vaunter's boast. They threw their arms around each other; they struggled on the plain. The earth is ploughed with their heels. Their bones crack as a boat on the ocean, when it leaps from wave to wave. Long did they toil; with night, they fell on the sounding plain; as two oaks, with their branches mingled, fall crashing from the hill. The tall son of Morny is bound; the aged overcame.

Fair with her locks of gold, her smooth neck, and her breasts of snow; fair, as the spirits of the hill when at silent noon they glide along the heath; fair, as the rainbow of heaven; came Minvane the maid. Fingal! she softly saith, loose me my brother Gaul. Loose me the hope of my race, the terror of all but Fingal. Can I, replies the king, can I deny the lovely daughter of the hill? Take thy brother, O Minvane, thou fairer than the snow of the north!

Such, Fingal! were thy words; but thy words I hear no more. Sightless I sit by thy tomb. I hear the wind in the wood; but no more I hear my friends. The cry of the hunter is over. The voice of war is ceased.

X   X

It is night; and I am alone, forlorn on the hill of storms. The wind is heard in the mountain. The torrent shrieks down the rock. No hut receives me from the rain; forlorn on the hill of winds.

Rise, moon! from behind thy clouds; stars of the night, appear! Lead me, some light, to the place where my love rests from the toil of the chace! his bow near him, unstrung; his dogs panting around him. But here I must sit alone, by the rock of the mossy stream. The stream and the wind roar; nor can I hear the voice of my love.

Why delayeth my Shalgar, why the son of the hill, his promise? Here is the rock and the tree. And here the roaring stream. Thou promisedst with night to be here. Ah! whither is my Shalgar gone? With thee I would fly my father; with thee, my brother of pride. Our race have long been foes; but we are not foes, O Shalgar!

Cease a little while, O wind! stream, be thou silent a while! let my voice be heard over the heath; let my wanderer hear me. Shalgar, it is I who call. Here is the tree, and the rock. Shalgar, my love! I am here. Why delayest thou thy coming? Alas! no answer.

Lo! the moon appeareth. The flood is bright in the vale. The rocks are grey on the face of the hill. But I see him not on the brow; his dogs before him tell not that he is coming. Here I must sit alone.

But who are these that lie beyond me on the heath? Are they my love and my brother? – Speak to me O my friends! they answer not. My soul is tormented with fears. – Ah! they are dead. Their swords are red from the fight. O my brother! my brother! why hast thou slain my Shalgar? why, O Shalgar! hast thou slain my brother? Dear were ye both to me! what shall I say in your praise? Thou wert fair on the hill among thousands; he was terrible in fight. Speak to me; hear my voice, sons of my love! But alas! they are silent; silent for ever! Cold are their breasts of clay!

Oh! from the rock of the hill; from the top of the mountain of winds, speak, ye ghosts of the dead! – Whither are ye gone to rest? In what cave of the hill shall I find you? No feeble voice is on the wind: no answer half-drowned in the storms of the hill.

I sit in my grief. I wait for morning in my tears. Rear the tomb, ye friends of the dead; but close it not till I come. My life flieth away like a dream: why should I stay behind? Here shall I rest with my friends by the stream of the sounding rock. When night comes on the hill; when the wind is upon the heath; my ghost shall stand in the wind, and mourn the death of my friends. The hunter shall hear from his booth. He shall fear, but love my voice. For sweet shall my voice be for my friends; for pleasant were they both to me.

PREFACE TO THE 1773 EDITION

Without encreasing his genius, the author may have improved his language, in the eleven years, that the following poems have been in the hands of the public. Errors in diction might have been committed at twenty-four, which the experience of a riper age may remove: and some exuberances in imagery may be restrained, with advantage, by a degree of judgement acquired in the progress of time. Impressed with this opinion, he ran over the whole with attention and accuracy; and, he hopes, he has brought the work to a state of correctness, which will preclude all future improvements . . .

The following poems, it must be confessed, are more calculated to please persons of exquisite feelings of heart, than those who receive all their impressions by the ear. The novelty of cadence, in what is called a prose version, though not destitute of harmony, will not to common readers supply the absence of the frequent returns of rhime. This was the opinion of the writer himself, tho' he yielded to the judgement of others, in a mode, which permitted freedom and dignity of expression, instead of fetters, which cramp the thought, whilst the harmony of language is preserved. His intention was to publish in verse. The making of poetry, like any other handicraft, may be learned by industry; and he has served his apprenticeship, though in secret, to the muses.

Genuine poetry, like gold, loses little when properly transfused; but when a composition cannot bear the test of a literal version, it is a counterfeit which ought not to pass current. The operation must, however, be performed with skilful hands. A translator, who cannot equal his original, is incapable of expressing its beauties.

Cath-Loda III

Whence is the stream of years? Whither do they roll along? Where have they hid, in mist, their many-coloured sides?

I look into the times of old, but they seem dim to Ossian's eyes, like reflected moon-beams on a distant lake. Here rise the red beams of war! There, silent, dwells a feeble race! They mark no years with their deeds, as slow they pass along. Dweller between the shields! thou that awakest the failing soul! descend from thy wall, harp of Cona, with thy voices three! Come with that which kindles the past: rear the forms of old, on their own dark-brown years!

Carric-thura

Hast thou left thy blue course in heaven, golden-haired son of the sky! The west has opened its gates, the bed of thy repose is there. The waves come to behold thy beauty. They lift their trembling heads. They see thee lovely in thy sleep; they shrink away with fear. Rest, in thy shady cave, O sun! let thy return be in joy.

But let a thousand lights arise to the sound of the harps of Selma: let the beam spread in the hall, the king of shells is returned! The strife of Carun is past, like sounds that are no more. Raise the song, O bards, the king is returned with his fame!

Dar-thula

Daughter of heaven, fair art thou! the silence of thy face is pleasant! Thou comest forth in loveliness. The stars attend thy blue course in the east. The clouds rejoice in thy presence, O moon: They brighten with dark-brown sides. Who is like thee in heaven, light of the silver night? The stars are ashamed in thy presence. They turn away their sparkling eyes. Whither dost thou retire from thy course, when the darkness of the countenance grows? Hast thou thy hall, like Ossian? Dwellest thou in the shadow of grief? Have thy sisters fallen from heaven? Are they who rejoiced with thee, at night, no more? Yes, they have fallen, fair light! and thou dost often retire to mourn. But thou thyself shalt fail, one night; and leave thy blue path in heaven. The stars

89

will then lift their heads: they, who were ashamed in they presence, will rejoice. Thou art now clothed with thy brightness. Look from thy gates in the sky. Burst the cloud, O wind, that the daughter of night may look forth! that the shaggy mountains may brighten, and the ocean roll its white waves, in light.

X   Oina-Morul

As flies the inconstant sun, over Larmon's grassy hill; so pass the tales of old, along my soul, by night! When bards are removed to their place, when harps are sung in Selma's hall; then comes a voice to Ossian, and awakes his soul! It is the voice of years that are gone! they roll before me, with all their deeds! I seize the tales, as they pass, and pour them forth in song. Nor a troubled stream is the song of the king, it is like the rising of music from Lutha of the strings. Lutha of many strings, not silent are thy streamy rocks, when the white hands of Malvina move upon the harp! Light of the shadowy thoughts, that fly across my soul, daughter of Toscar of helmets, wilt thou not hear the song! We call back, maid of Lutha, the years that have rolled away.

The War of Caros

Bring, daughter of Toscar, bring the harp! the light of the song rises in Ossian's soul! It is like the field, when darkness covers the hills around, and the shadow grows slowly on the plain of the sun. I behold my son, O Malvina, near the mossy rock of Crona. But it is the mist of the desert, tinged with the beam of the west! Lovely is the mist that assumes the form of Oscar! turn from it, ye winds, when ye roar on the side of Ardven!

Cathlin of Clutha

Come, thou beam that art lonely, from watching in the night! The squally winds are around thee, from all their echoing hills. Red, over my hundred streams, are the light-covered paths of the dead. They rejoice, on the eddying winds, in the still season of night. Dwells there no joy in song, white hand of the harps of Lutha? Awake the voice of the string; and roll my soul to me. It is a stream that has failed. Malvina, pour the song.

I hear thee, from thy darkness, in Selma, thou that watchest, lonely, by night! Why didst thou with-hold the song, from Ossian's failing soul? As the falling brook to the ear of the hunter, descending from his storm-covered hill; in a sun-beam rolls the echoing stream; he hears, and shakes his dewy locks: such is the voice of Lutha, to the friend of the spirits of heroes. My swelling bosom beats high. I look back on the days that are past. Come thou beam that art lonely, from watching in the night!

Oithona

Darkness dwells around Dunlathmon, though the moon shews half her face on the hill. The daughter of night turns her eyes away; she beholds the approaching grief. The son of Morven is on the plain: there is no sound in the hall. No long-streaming beam of light comes trembling through the gloom. The voice of Oithona is not heard amidst the noise of the streams of Duvranna. 'Whither art thou gone in thy beauty, dark-haired daughter of Nuath? Lathmon is in the field of the valiant, but thou didst promise to remain in the hall; thou didst promise to remain in the hall till the son of Morni returned. Till he returned from Strumon, to the maid of his love! the tear was on thy cheek at his departure; the sigh rose in secret in thy breast. But thou dost not come forth with songs, with the lightly-trembling sound of the harp!'

Such were the words of Gaul, when he came to Dunlathmon's towers. The gates were open and dark. The winds were blustering in the hall. The trees strowed the threshold with leaves; the murmur of night was abroad. Sad and silent, at a rock, the son of Morni sat: his soul trembled for the maid; but he knew not whither to turn his course! The son of Leth stood at a distance, and heard the winds in his bushy hair. But he did not raise his voice, for he saw the sorrow of Gaul!

Sleep descended on the chiefs. The visions of night arose. Oithona stood, in a dream, before the eyes of Morni's son. Her hair was loose and disordered: her lovely eye rolled deep in tears. Blood stained her snowy arm. The robe half hid the wound in her breast. She stood over the chief, and her voice was feebly heard. 'Sleeps the son of Morni, he that was lovely in the eyes of Oithona?

Sleeps Gaul at the distant rock, and the daughter of Nuath low? The sea rolls round the dark isle of Tromathon. I sit in my tears in the cave! Nor do I sit alone, O Gaul, the dark chief of Cuthal is there. He is there in the rage of his love. What can Oithona do?'

A rougher blast rushed through the oak. The dream of night departed. Gaul took his aspen spear. He stood in the rage of his soul. Often did his eyes turn to the east. He accused the lagging light. At length the morning came forth. The hero lifted up the sail. The winds came rustling from the hill; he bounded on the waves of the deep. On the third day arose Tromathon, like a blue shield in the midst of the sea. The white wave roared against its rocks; sad Oithona sat on the coast! She looked on the rolling waters, and her tears came down. But when she saw Gaul in his arms, she started and turned her eyes away. Her lovely cheek is bent and red; her white arm trembles by her side. Thrice she strove to fly from his presence; thrice her steps failed her as she went!

'Daughter of Nuath,' said the hero, 'why dost thou fly from Gaul? Do my eyes send forth the flame of death? Darkens hatred on my soul? Thou art to me the beam of the east, rising in a land unknown. But thou coverest thy face with sadness, daughter of car-borne Nuath! Is the foe of Oithona near? My soul burns to meet him in fight. The sword trembles by the side of Gaul, and longs to glitter in his hand. Speak, daughter of Nuath, dost thou not behold my tears!'

'Young chief of Strumon,' replied the maid, 'why comest thou over the dark-blue wave, to Nuath's mournful daughter? Why did I not pass away in secret, like the flower of the rock, that lifts its fair head unseen, and strows its withered leaves on the blast? Why didst thou come, O Gaul, to hear my departing sigh? I vanish in my youth; my name shall not be heard. Or it will be heard with grief; the tears of Nuath must fall. Thou wilt be sad, son of Morni, for the departed fame of Oithona. But she shall sleep in the narrow tomb, far from the voice of the mourner. Why didst thou come, chief of Strumon, to the sea-beat rocks of Tromathon?'

'I came to meet thy foes, daughter of car-borne Nuath! the death of Cuthal's chief darkens before me; or Morni's son shall fall! Oithona! when Gaul is low, raise my tomb on that oozy rock. When the dark-bounding ship shall pass, call the sons of the sea! call them, and give this sword, to bear it hence to Morni's hall. The gray-haired chief will then cease to look toward the desert, for the return of his son!'

'Shall the daughter of Nuath live?' she replied with a bursting sigh. 'Shall I live in Tromathon, and the son of Morni low? My heart is not of that rock; nor my soul careless as that sea; which lifts its blue waves to every wind, and rolls beneath the storm! The blast which shall lay thee low, shall spread the branches of Oithona on earth. We shall wither together, son of car-borne Morni! The narrow house is pleasant to me, and the grey stone of the dead, for never more will I leave thy rocks, O sea-surrounded Tromathon! Night came on with her clouds after the departure of Lathmon, when he went to the wars of his fathers, to the moss-covered rock of Duthormoth. Night came on. I sat in the hall, at the beam of the oak! The wind was abroad in the trees. I heard the sound of arms. Joy rose in my face. I thought of thy return. It was the chief of Cuthal, the red-haired strength of Dunrommath. His eyes rolled in fire: the blood of my people was on his sword. They who defended Oithona fell by the gloomy chief! What could I do? My arm was weak. I could not lift the spear. He took me in my grief, amidst my tears he raised the sail. He feared the returning Lathmon, the brother of unhappy Oithona! But behold he comes with his people! the dark wave is divided before him! Whither wilt thou turn thy steps, son of Morni? Many are the warriors of thy foe!'

'My steps never turned from battle,' Gaul said and unsheathed his sword. 'Shall I then begin to fear, Oithona, when thy foes are near? Go to thy cave, my love, till our battle cease on the field. Son of Leth, bring the bows of our fathers! the sounding quiver of Morni! Let our three warriors bend the yew. Ourselves will lift the spear. They are an host on the rock! our souls are strong in war!'

Oithona went to the cave. A troubled joy rose on her mind, like the red path of lightning on a stormy cloud! Her soul was resolved; the tear was dried from her wildly-looking eye. Dunrommath slowly approached. He saw the son of Morni. Contempt contracted his face, a smile is on his dark-brown cheek; his red eye rolled, half-concealed, beneath his shaggy brows!

'Whence are the sons of the sea,' begun the gloomy chief? 'Have the winds driven you on the rocks of Tromathon? Or come you in search of the white-handed maid? The sons of the unhappy, ye feeble men, come to the hand of Dunrommath! His eye spares not the weak; he delights in the blood of strangers. Oithona is a beam of light, and the chief of Cuthal enjoys it in secret; wouldst thou come on its loveliness, like a cloud, son of the feeble hand! Thou mayst come, but shalt thou return to the halls of thy fathers?' 'Dost thou not know me,' said Gaul, 'red-haired chief of Cuthal? Thy feet were swift on the heath, in the battle of car-borne Lathmon; when the sword of Morni's son pursued his host, in Morven's woody land. Dunrommath! thy words are mighty, for thy warriors gather behind thee. But do I fear them, son of pride? I am not of the race of the feeble!'

Gaul advanced in his arms; Dunrommath shrunk behind his people. But the spear of Gaul pierced the gloomy chief; his sword lopped off his head, as it bended in death. The son of Morni shook it thrice by the lock; the warriors of Dunrommath fled. The arrows of Morven pursued them: ten fell on the mossy rocks. The rest lift the sounding sail, and bound on the troubled deep. Gaul advanced towards the cave of Oithona. He beheld a youth leaning on a rock. An arrow had pierced his side; his eye rolled faintly beneath his helmet. The soul of Morni's son was sad, he came and spoke the words of peace.

'Can the hand of Gaul heal thee, youth of the mournful brow? I have searched for the herbs of the mountains; I have gathered them on the secret banks of their streams. My hand has closed the wound of the brave, their eyes have blessed the son of Morni. Where dwelt thy fathers, warrior? Were they of the sons of the mighty? Sadness shall come, like night, on thy native stream. Thou art fallen in thy youth!'

'My fathers,' replied the youth, 'were of the race of the mighty; but they shall not be sad; for my fame is departed like mountain mist. High walls rise on the banks of Duvranna; and see their mossy towers in the stream; a rock ascends behind them with its bending pines. Thou mayst behold it far distant. There my brother dwells. He is renowned in battle: give him this glittering helm!

The helmet fell from the hand of Gaul. It was the wounded Oithona! She had armed herself in the cave, and came in search of death. Her heavy eyes are half closed; the blood pours from her heaving side. 'Son of Morni,' she said, 'prepare the narrow tomb. Sleep grows, like darkness, on my soul. The eyes of Oithona are dim! O had I dwelt at Duvranna, in the bright beam of my fame! then had my years come on with joy; the virgins would then bless my steps. But I fall in youth, son of Morni; my father shall blush in his hall!'

She fell pale on the rock of Tromathon. The mournful warrior raised her tomb. He came to Morven; we saw the darkness of his soul. Ossian took the harp in praise of Oithona. The brightness of the face of Gaul returned. But his sigh rose, at times, in the midst of his friends; like blasts that shake their unfrequent wings, after the stormy winds are laid!

Carthon

'Tell,' said the mighty Fingal, 'the tale of thy youthful days. Sorrow, like a cloud on the sun shades the soul of Clessammor. Mournful are thy thoughts, alone, on the banks of the roaring Lora. Let us hear the sorrow of thy youth, and the darkness of thy days!'

'It was in the days of peace,' replied the great Clessammor, 'I came, in my bounding ship, to Balclutha's wall of towers. The winds had roared behind my sails, and Clutha's streams received my dark-bosomed ship. Three days I remained in Reuthamir's halls and saw his daughter, that beam of light. The joy of the shell went round, and the aged hero gave the fair. Her breasts were like foam on the wave, and her eyes like stars of light: her hair was dark as the raven's wing: her soul was generous and mild. My love for Moina was great: my heart poured forth in joy.

'The son of a stranger came; a chief who loved the white-bosomed Moina. His words were mighty in the hall; he often

95

half-unsheathed his sword. Where, said he, is the mighty Comhal, the restless wanderer of the heath? Comes he, with his host, to Balclutha, since Clessammor is so bold? My soul, I replied, O warrior! burns in a light of its own. I stand without fear in the midst of thousands, though the valiant are distant far. Stranger! thy words are mighty; for Clessammor is alone. But my sword trembles by my side, and longs to glitter in my hand. Speak no more of Comhal, son of the winding Clutha!

'The strength of his pride arose. We fought; he fell beneath my sword. The banks of Clutha heard his fall; a thousand spears glittered around. I fought: the strangers prevailed: I plunged into the stream of Clutha. My white sails rose over the waves, and I bounded on the dark-blue sea. Moina came to the shore, and rolled the red eye of her tears: her loose hair flew on the wind; and I heard her mournful, distant cries. Often did I turn my ship! but the winds of the east prevailed. Nor Clutha ever since have I seen, nor Moina of the dark brown hair. She fell in Balclutha; for I have seen her ghost. I knew her as she came through the dusky night, along the murmur of Lora: she was like the new moon, seen through the gathered mist: when the sky pours down its flaky snow, and the world is silent and dark.'

'Raise, ye bards', said the mighty Fingal, 'the praise of unhappy Moina. Call her ghost, with your songs, to our hills; that she may rest with the fair of Morven, the sun-beams of other days, the delight of heroes of old. I have seen the walls of Balclutha, but they were desolate. The fire had resounded in the halls: and the voice of the people is heard no more. The stream of Clutha was removed from its place by the fall of the walls. The thistle shook, there, its lonely head: the moss whistled to the wind. The fox looked out, from the windows, the rank grass of the wall waved round its head. Desolate is the dwelling of Moina, silence is in the house of her fathers. Raise the song of mourning, O bards, over the land of strangers. They have but fallen before us: for, one day, we must fall. Why dost thou build the hall, son of the winged days? Thou lookest from thy towers to-day; yet a few years, and the blast of the desart comes; it howls in thy empty court, and whistles round thy half-worn shield. And let the blast of the desart come, we shall be renowned in our day! The mark of my arm shall be in battle; my name in the song of bards. Raise the song; send round the shell: let joy be heard in my hall. When thou, sun of heaven, shalt fail! if thou shalt fail, thou mighty light! if thy brightness is for a season, like Fingal, our fame shall survive thy beams!'

*

Fingal beheld the hero's blood; he stopt the uplifted spear. 'Yield, king of swords!' said Comhal's son; 'I behold thy blood. Thou hast been mighty in battle; and thy fame shall never fade.' 'Art thou the king so far renowned,' replied the car-borne Carthon? 'Art thou that light of death, that frightens the kings of the world? But why should Carthon ask? for he is like the stream of his hills; strong as a river, in his course: swift as the eagle of heaven. O that I had fought with the king; that my fame might be great in song! that the hunter, beholding my tomb, might say, he fought with the mighty Fingal. But Carthon dies unknown; he has poured out his force on the weak.'

But thou shalt not die unknown,' replied the king of woody Morven; 'my bards are many, O Carthon, their songs descend to future times. The children of years to come shall hear the fame of Carthon; when they sit round the burning oak, and the night is spent in songs of old. The hunter, sitting in the heath, shall hear the rustling blast; and, raising his eyes, behold the rock where Carthon fell. He shall turn to his son, and show the place where the mighty fought; 'There the king of Balclutha fought, like the strength of a thousand streams.'

Joy rose in Carthon's face; he lifted his heavy eyes...

Croma

I raised my voice for Fovar-gormo, when they laid the chief on earth. The aged Crothar was there, but his sigh was not heard. He searched for the wound of his son, and found it in his breast. Joy rose in the face of the aged. He came and spoke to Ossian. 'King of spears!' he said, 'my son has not fallen without his fame. The young warrior did not fly; but met death, as he went forward in his strength. Happy are they who die in youth, when their renown is heard! The feeble will not behold them in the hall; or smile at their trembling hands. Their memory shall be honoured in song; the young tear of the virgin will fall. But the aged wither away, by degrees; the fame of their youth, while they yet live, is all forgot. They fall in secret. The sigh of their son is not heard. Joy is around their tomb; the stone of their fame is placed without a tear. Happy are they who die in youth, when their renown is around them.'

Colna-Dona

Beneath the voice of the king, we moved to Crona of the streams, Toscar of grassy Lutha, and Ossian, young in fields. Three bards attended with songs. Three bossy shields were borne before us; for we were to rear the stone, in memory of the past. By Crona's mossy course, Fingal had scattered his foes: he had rolled away the strangers, like a troubled sea. We came to the place of renown; from the mountains descended night. I tore an oak from its hill, and raised a flame on high. I bade my fathers to look down, from the clouds of their hall; for, at the fame of their race, they brighten in the wind.

I took a stone from the stream, amidst the song of bards. The blood of Fingal's foes hung curdled in its ooze. Beneath, I placed, at intervals, three bosses from the shields of foes, as rose or fell the sound of Ullin's nightly song. Toscar laid a dagger in earth, a mail of sounding steel. We raised the mould around the stone, and bade it speak to other years.

'Oozy daughter of streams, that now art reared on high, speak to the feeble, O stone, after Selma's race have failed! Prone, from the stormy night, the traveller shall lay him, by thy side: thy whistling moss shall sound in his dreams; the years that were past shall return. Battles rise before him, blue-shielded kings descend to war: the darkened moon looks from heaven, on the troubled field. He shall burst, with morning, from dreams, and see the tombs of warriors round. He shall ask about the stone; and the aged shall reply, "This grey stone was raised by Ossian, a chief of other years!"'

Fingal III

As a hundred winds on Morven; as the streams of a hundred hills; as clouds fly successive over heaven; as the dark ocean assails the shore of the desert: so roaring, so vast, so terrible the armies mixed on Lena's echoing heath. The groan of the people spread over the hills: it was like the thunder of night, when the cloud bursts on Cona, and a thousand ghosts shriek at once on the hollow wind. Fingal rushed on in his strength, terrible as the spirit of Trenmor; when, in a whirlwind, he comes to Morven, to see the children of his pride. The oaks resound on their mountains, and their rocks fall down before him. Dimly seen, as lightens the night, he strides largely from hill to hill. Bloody was the hand of my father, when he whirled the gleam of his sword. He remembers the battles of his youth. The field is wasted in the course!

Ryno went on like a pillar of fire. Dark is the brow of Gaul. Fergus rushed forward with feet of wind. Fillan, like the mist of the hill. Ossian, like a rock, came down. I exulted in the strength of the king. Many were the deaths of my arm! dismal the gleam of my sword! My locks were not then so grey; nor trembled my hands with age. My eyes were not closed in darkness; my feet failed not in the race.

Who can relate the deaths of his people? Who the deeds of mighty heroes?...

✕ Fingal V

But behold the king of Morven! He moves, below, like a pillar of fire. His strength is like the stream of Lubar, or the wind of echoing Cromla; when the branchy forests of night are torn from all their rocks! Happy are thy people, O Fingal! thine arm shall finish their wars. Thou art the first in their dangers: the wisest in the days of their peace. Thou speakest and thy thousands obey: armies tremble at the sound of thy steel. Happy are thy people, O Fingal, king of resounding Selma! Who is that so dark and terrible, coming in the thunder of his course? who, but Starno's son to meet the king of Morven? Behold the battle of the chiefs! it is the storm of the ocean, when two spirits meet far distant, and contend

99

for the rolling of waves. The hunter hears the noise on his hill. He sees the high billows advancing to Ardven's shore!

Such were the winds of Connal, when the heroes met, in fight. There was a clang of arms! There every blow, like the hundred hammers of the furnace! Terrible is the battle of the kings; dreadful the look of their eyes. Their dark-brown shields are cleft in twain. Their steel flies, broken, from their helms. They fling their weapons down. Each rushes to his hero's grasp. Their sinewy arms bend round each other; they turn from side to side, and strain and stretch their large spreading limbs below. But when the pride of their strength arose, they shook the hill with their heels. Rocks tumble from their places on high; the green-shaded bushes are overturned. At length the strength of Swaran fell. The king of the groves is bound. Thus have I seen on Cona; but Cona I behold no more! thus have I seen two dark hills, removed from their place, by the strength of the bursting stream. They turn from side to side in their fall; their tall oaks meet one another on high. Then they tumble together with all their rocks and trees. The streams are turned by their side. The red ruin is seen afar.

✕ *Fingal* VI

'Youth of the feeble arm,' said Fingal, 'Connan, cease thy words! Cuthullin is renowned in battle; terrible over the world. Often have I heard thy fame, thou stormy chief of Inis-fail. Spread now thy white sails for the isle of mist. See Bragela leaning on her rock. Her tender eye is in tears; the winds lift her long hair from her heaving breast. She listens to the breeze of night, to hear the voice of thy rowers; to hear the song of the sea! the sound of thy distant harp!'

'Long shall she listen in vain. Cuthullin shall never return! How can I behold Bragela, to raise the sigh of her breast? Fingal, I was always victorious in battles of other spears!' 'And hereafter thou shalt be victorious,' said Fingal of generous shells. 'The fame of Cuthullin shall grow, like the branchy tree of Cromla. Many battles await thee, O chief! Many shall be the wounds of thy hand! Bring hither, Oscar, the deer! Prepare the feast of shells. Let our souls rejoice after danger, and our friends delight in our presence!'

We sat. We feasted. We sung. The soul of Cuthullin rose. The strength of his arm returned. Gladness brightened along his face. Ullin gave the song; Carril raised the voice. I joined the bards, and sung of battles of the spear. Battles! where I often fought. Now I fight no more! The fame of my former deeds is ceased. I sit forlorn at the tombs of my friends!

Thus the night passed away in song. We brought back the morning with joy. Fingal arose on the heath, and shook his glittering spear. He moved first toward the plains of Lena. We followed in all our arms.

'Spread the sail,' said the king, 'seize the winds as they pour from Lena.' We rose on the waves with songs. We rushed, with joy, through the foam of the deep.

Temora VIII

'Why speaks the king of the tomb? Ossian! the warrior has failed! Joy meet thy soul, like a stream, Cathmor, friend of strangers! My son, I hear the call of years; they take my spear as they pass along. Why does not Fingal, they seem to say, rest within his hall? Dost thou always delight in blood? In the tear of the sad? No: ye dark-rolling years, Fingal delights not in blood. Tears are wintry streams that waste away my soul. But, when I lie down to rest, then comes the mighty voice of war. It awakes me, in my hall, and calls forth all my steel. It shall call forth no more; Ossian, take thou my father's spear. Lift it, in battle, when the proud arise.

'My fathers, Ossian, trace my steps; my deeds are pleasant to their eyes. Wherever I come forth to battle, on my field, are their columns of mist. But mine arm rescued the feeble; the haughty found my rage was fire. Never over the fallen did mine eye rejoice. For this, my fathers shall meet me, at the gates of their airy halls, tall, with robes of light, with mildly-kindled eyes. But, to the proud in arms, they are darkened moons on heaven, which send the fire of night, red-wandering over their face.

'Father of heroes, Trenmor, dweller of eddying winds! I give thy spear to Ossian, let thine eye rejoice. Thee have I seen, at times, bright from between the clouds; so appear to my son, when he is to lift the spear: then shall he remember thy mighty deeds, though thou art now but a blast.'

He gave the spear to my hand, and raised at once a stone on high, to speak to future times, with its grey head of moss. Beneath he placed a sword in earth, and one bright boss from his shield. Dark in thought, a-while, he bends: his words, at length, came forth.

'When thou, O stone, shalt moulder down, and lose thee, in the moss of years, then shall the traveller come, and whistling, pass away. Thou knowest not, feeble man, that fame once shone on Moi-lena. Here Fingal resigned his spear, after the last of his fields. Pass away, thou empty shade; in thy voice there is no renown. Thou dwellest by some peaceful stream; yet a few years, and thou art gone. No one remembers thee, thou dweller of thick mist! But Fingal shall be clothed with fame, a beam of light to other times; for he went forth, in echoing steel, to save the weak in arms.'

Carric-thura

Night came down on the sea; Rotha's bay received the ship. A rock bends along the coast with all its echoing wood. On the top is the circle of Loda, the mossy stone of power! A narrow plain spreads beneath, covered with grass and aged trees, which the midnight winds, in their wrath, had torn from the shaggy rock. The blue course of a stream is there! the lonely blast of ocean pursues the thistle's beard! The flame of three oaks arose; the feast is spread around: but the soul of the king is sad, for Carric-Thura's chief distrest.

The wan, cold moon rose, in the east. Sleep descended on the youths! Their blue helmets glitter to the beam; the fading fire decays. But sleep did not rest on the king; he rose in the midst of his arms, and slowly ascended the hill to behold the flame of Sarno's tower.

The flame was dim and distant; the moon hid her red face in the east. A blast came from the mountain; on its wings was the spirit of Loda. He came to his place in his terrors, and shook his dusky spear. His eyes appeared like flames in his dark face; his voice is

102

like distant thunder. Fingal advanced his spear in night, and raised his voice on high.

'Son of night retire: call thy winds and fly! Why dost thou come to my presence, with thy shadowy arms? Do I fear thy gloomy form, spirit of dismal Loda? Weak is thy shield of clouds; feeble is that meteor, thy sword. The blast rolls them together; and thou thyself art lost. Fly from my presence, son of night! call thy winds and fly!'

'Dost thou force me from my place?' replied the hollow voice. 'The people bend before me. I turn the battle in the field of the brave. I look on the nations and they vanish: my nostrils pour the blast of death. I come abroad on the winds: the tempests are before my face. But my dwelling is calm, above the clouds; the fields of my rest are pleasant.'

'Dwell in thy pleasant fields,' said the king. 'Let Comhal's son be forgot. Do my steps ascend from my hills, into thy peaceful plains? Do I meet thee with a spear, on thy cloud, spirit of dismal Loda? Why then dost thou frown on me? why shake thine airy spear? Thou frownest in vain: I never fled from the mighty in war. And shall the sons of the wind frighten the king of Morven? No: he knows the weakness of their arms!'

'Fly to thy land,' replied the form: 'receive the wind and fly! The blasts are in the hollow of my hand: the course of the storm is mine. The king of Sora is my son, he bends at the stone of my power. His battle is around Carric-thura; and he will prevail! Fly to thy land, son of Comhal, or feel my flaming wrath!'

He lifted high his shadowy spear! He bent forward his dreadful height. Fingal, advancing, drew his sword; the blade of dark-brown Luno. The gleaming path of the steel winds through the gloomy ghost. The form fell shapeless into air, like a column of smoke, which the staff of the boy disturbs, as it rises from the half-extinguished furnace.

The spirit of Loda shrieked, as, rolled into himself, he rose on the wind. Inistore shook at the sound. The waves heard it on the deep. They stopped in their course with fear: the friends of Fingal started, at once; they took their heavy spears. They missed the king; they rose in rage; all their arms resound.

103

The moon came forth in the east. Fingal returned in the gleam of his arms. The joy of his youth was great, their souls settled, as a sea from a storm. Ullin raised the song of gladness. The hills of Inistore rejoiced. The flame of the oak arose; and the tales of heroes are told.

*

Three days feasted the kings: on the fourth their white sails arose. The winds of the north drove Fingal to Morven's woody land. But the spirit of Loda sat, in his cloud, behind the ships of Frothal. He hung forward with all his blasts, and spread the white-bosomed sails. The wounds of his form were not forgot; he still feared the hand of the king.

Fingal II

Connal lay by the sound of the mountain stream, beneath the aged tree. A stone, with its moss, supported his head. Shrill through the heath of Lena, he heard the voice of night. At distance from the heroes he lay; the son of the sword feared no foe! The hero beheld, in his rest, a dark-red stream of fire rushing down from the hill. Crugal sat upon the beam, a chief who fell in fight. He fell by the hand of Swaran, striving in the battle of heroes. His face is like the beam of the setting moon. His robes are of the clouds of the hill. His eyes are two decaying flames! Dark is the wound of his breast! 'Crugal,' said the mighty Connal, 'son of Dedgal famed on the hill of hinds! Why so pale and sad, thou breaker of the shields? Thou hast never been pale for fear! What disturbs the departed Crugal?' Dim, and in tears, he stood, and stretched his pale hand over the hero. Faintly he raised his feeble voice, like the gale of the reedy Lego!

'My spirit, Connal, is on my hills: my corse on the sands of Erin. Thou shalt never talk with Crugal, nor find his lone steps in the heath. I am light as the blast of Cromla. I move like the shadow of mist! Connal, son of Colgar, I see a cloud of death: it hovers dark over the plains of Lena. The sons of green Erin must fall. Remove from the field of ghosts.' Like the darkened moon he retired, in the midst of the whistling blast. 'Stay,' said the mighty Connal, 'stay, my dark-red friend. Lay by that beam of heaven, son of the windy Cromla! What cave is thy lonely house? What green-headed hill the place of thy repose? Shall we not hear thee in the storm? In the noise of the mountain-stream? When the feeble sons of the wind come forth, and scarcely seen, pass over the desert?'

The soft-voiced Connal rose, in the midst of his sounding arms. He struck his shield above Cuthullin. The son of battle waked. 'Why', said the ruler of the car, 'comes Connal through my night? My spear might turn against the sound; and Cuthullin mourn the death of his friend. Speak, Connal; son of Colgar, speak, thy council is the sun of heaven! 'Son of Semo!' replied the chief, 'the ghost of Crugal came from his cave. The stars dim-twinkled through his form. His voice was like the sound of a distant stream. He is a messenger of death! He speaks of the dark and narrow house! Sue for peace, O chief of Erin! or fly over the heath of Lena.'

'He spoke to Connal,' replied the hero, 'though stars dim-twinkled through his form! Son of Colgar, it was the wind that murmured across thy ear. Or if it was the form of Crugal, why didst thou not force him to my sight? Hast thou enquired where is his cave? The house of that son of wind? My sword might find that voice, and force his knowledge from Crugal. But small is his knowledge, Connal; he was here to-day. He could not have gone beyond our hills! who could tell him there of our fall?' 'Ghosts fly on clouds, and ride on winds,' said Connal's voice of wisdom. 'They rest together in their caves, and talk of mortal men.'

'Then let them talk of mortal men; of every man but Erin's chief. Let me be forgot in their cave. I will not fly from Swaran! If fall I must, my tomb shall rise, amidst the fame of future times. The hunter shall shed a tear on my stone; sorrow shall dwell round the high-bosomed Bragela. I fear not death, to fly I fear! Fingal has seen me victorious! Thou dim phantom of the hill, shew thyself to me! come on thy beam of heaven, shew me my death in thine hand; yet I will not fly, thou feeble son of the wind!

Go, son of Colgar, strike the shield. It hangs between the spears.
Let my warriors rise to the sound, in the midst of the battles of
Erin. Though Fingal delays his coming with the race of the stormy
isles; we shall fight, O Colgar's son, and die in the battle of
heroes!'

Berrathon

Malvina! where art thou, with thy songs, with the soft sound of
thy steps? Son of Alpin, art thou near? where is the daughter of
Toscar? 'I passed, O son of Fingal, by Tor-lutha's mossy walls.
The smoke of the hall was ceased. Silence was among the trees of
the hill. The voice of the chace was over. I saw the daughters of
the bow. I asked about Malvina, but they answered not. They
turned their faces away: thin darkness covered their beauty. They
were like stars, on a rainy hill, by night, each looking faintly
through the mist.'

Pleasant be thy rest, O lovely beam! soon hast thou set on our
hills! The steps of thy departure were stately, like the moon on
the blue-trembling wave. But thou hast left us in darkness, first of
the maids of Lutha! We sit, at the rock, and there is no voice; no
light but the meteor of fire! Soon hast thou set, O Malvina, daugh-
ter of generous Toscar! But thou risest like the beam of the east,
among the spirits of thy friends, where they sit, in their stormy
halls, the chambers of the thunder. A cloud hovers over Cona. Its
blue curling sides are high. The winds are beneath it, with their
wings. Within it is the dwelling of Fingal. There the hero sits in
darkness. His airy spear is in his hand. His shield half covered
with clouds, is like the darkened moon; when one half still
remains in the wave, and the other looks sickly on the field!

His friends sit around the king, on mist! They hear the songs of
Ullin: he strikes the half-viewless harp. He raises the feeble voice.
The lesser heroes, with a thousand meteors, light the airy hall.
Malvina rises, in the midst; a blush is on her cheek. She beholds
the unknown faces of her fathers. She turns aside her humid
eyes. 'Art thou come too soon?' said Fingal, 'daughter of gener-
ous Toscar. Sadness dwells in the hall of Lutha, My aged son is

106

sad! I hear the breeze of Cona, that was wont to lift thy heavy locks. It comes to the hall, but thou art not there. Its voice is mournful among the arms of thy fathers! Go, with thy rustling wing, O breeze! sigh on Malvina's tomb. It rises yonder beneath the rock, at the blue stream of Lutha. The maids are departed to their place. Thou alone, O breeze, mournest there!'

*

Such were my deeds, son of Alpin, when the arm of my youth was strong. Such the actions of Toscar, the car-borne son of Conloch. But Toscar is on his flying cloud. I am alone at Lutha. My voice is like the last sound of the wind, when it forsakes the woods. But Ossian shall not be long alone. He sees the mist that shall receive his ghost. He beholds the mist that shall from his robe, when he appears on his hills. The sons of feeble men shall behold me, and admire the stature of the chiefs of old. They shall creep to their caves. They shall look to the sky with fear: for my steps shall be in the clouds. Darkness shall roll on my side.

Lead, son of Alpin, lead the aged to his woods. The winds begin to rise. The dark wave of the lake resounds. Bends there not a tree from Mora with its branches bare? It bends, son of Alpin, in the rustling blast. My harp hangs on a blasted branch. The sound of its strings is mournful. Does the wind touch thee, O harp, or is it some passing ghost! It is the hand of Malvina! Bring me the harp, son of Alpin. Another song shall rise. My soul shall depart in the sound. My fathers shall hear it in their airy hall. Their dim faces shall hang, with joy, from their clouds; and their hands receive their son. The aged oak bends over the stream. It sighs with all its moss. The withered fern whistles near, and mixes, as it waves, with Ossian's hair.

'Strike the harp, and raise the song: be near, with all your wings, ye winds. Bear the mournful sound away to Fingal's airy hall. Bear it to Fingal's hall, that he may hear the voice of his son. The voice of him that praised the mighty!'

'The blast of the north opens thy gates, O king. I behold thee sitting on mist, dimly gleaming in all thine arms. Thy form now is not the terror of the valiant. It is like a watery cloud; when we

107

see stars behind it, with their weeping eyes. Thy shield is the aged moon; thy sword a vapour half-kindled with fire. Dim and feeble is the chief, who travelled in brightness before! But thy steps are on the winds of the desert. The storms are darkening in thy hand. Thou takest the sun in thy wrath, and hidest him in thy clouds. The sons of little men are afraid. A thousand showers descend. But when thou comest forth in thy mildness, the gale of the morning is near thy course. The sun laughs in his blue fields. The grey stream winds in its vale. The bushes shake their green heads in the wind. The roes bound toward the desert.'

'There is a murmur in the heath! the stormy winds abate! I hear the voice of Fingal. Long has it been absent from mine ear! "Come, Ossian, come away," he says. Fingal has received his fame. We passed away, like flames that had shone for a season. Our departure was in renown. Though the plains of our battles are dark and silent; our fame is in the four grey stones. The voice of Ossian has been heard. The harp has been strung in Selma. "Come, Ossian, come away," he says, "come, fly with thy fathers on clouds." I come, I come, thou king of men! The life of Ossian fails. I begin to vanish on Cona. My steps are not seen in Selma. Beside the stone of Mora I shall fall asleep. The winds whistling in my grey hair, shall not awaken me. Depart, on thy wings, O wind: thou canst not disturb the rest of the bard. The night is long, but his eyes are heavy. Depart, thou rustling blast.'

'But why art thou sad, son of Fingal? Why grows the cloud of thy soul? The chiefs of other times are departed. They have gone without their fame. The sons of future years shall pass away. Another race shall arise. The people are like the waves of ocean: like the leaves of woody Morven, they pass away in the rustling blast, and other leaves lift their green heads on high.'

Did thy beauty last, O Ryno! Stood the strength of car-borne Oscar? Fingal himself departed. The halls of his fathers forgot his steps. Shalt thou then remain, thou aged bard! when the mighty have failed? But my fame shall remain, and grow like the oak of Morven; which lifts its broad head to the storm, and rejoices in the course of the wind!

The War of Caros

Darkness comes on my soul, O fair daughter of Toscar, I behold not the form of my son at Carun; nor the figure of Oscar on Crona. The rustling winds have carried him far away; and the heart of his father is sad. But lead me, O Malvina, to the sound of my woods; to the roar of my mountain streams. Let the chace be heard on Cona; let me think on the days of other years. And bring me the harp, O maid, that I may touch it, when the light of my soul shall arise. Be thou near, to learn the song; future times shall hear of me! The sons of the feeble hereafter will lift the voice on Cona; and looking up to the rocks, say, 'Here Ossian dwelt'. They shall admire the chiefs of old, the race that are no more! while we ride on our clouds, Malvina, on the wings of the roaring winds. Our voices shall be heard, at times, in the desert; we shall sing on the breeze of the rock.

✕ Carthon

Fingal was sad for Carthon; he commanded his bards to mark the day, when shadowy autumn returned... Ossian often joined their voice; and added to their song. 'My soul has been mournful for Carthon; he fell in the days of his youth: and thou, O Clessamor! where is thy dwelling in the wind? Has the youth forgot his wound? Flies he, on clouds, with thee? I feel the sun, O Malvina, leave me to my rest. Perhaps they may come to my dreams; I think I hear a feeble voice! The beam of heaven delights to shine on the grave of Carthon: I feel it warm around!

'O thou that rollest above, round as the shield of my fathers! Whence are thy beams, O sun! thy everlasting light? Thou comest forth, in thy awful beauty; the stars hide themselves in the sky; the moon, cold and pale, sinks in the western wave. But thou thyself movest alone; who can be a companion of thy course! The oaks of the mountains fall; the mountains themselves decay with years; the ocean shrinks and grows again; the moon herself is lost in heaven: but thou art for ever the same; rejoicing in the brightness of thy course. When the world is dark with tempests; when thunder rolls, and lightning flies; thou lookest in thy beauty, from the clouds, and laughest at the storm. But to Ossian, thou lookest in vain; for he beholds thy beams no more; whether thy yellow hair flows on the eastern clouds, or thou tremblest at the gates of the west. But thou art perhaps, like me, for a season, thy years will have an end. Thou shalt sleep in the clouds, careless of the voice of the morning. Exult then, O sun, in the strength of thy youth! Age is dark and unlovely; it is like the glimmering light of the moon, when it shines through broken clouds, and the mist is on the hills; the blast of north is on the plain, the traveller shrinks in the midst of his journey.'

The Songs of Selma

Star of descending night! fair is thy light in the west! thou liftest thy unshorn head from thy cloud: thy steps are stately on thy hill. What dost thou behold in the plain? The stormy winds are laid. The murmur of the torrent comes from afar. Roaring waves climb the distant rock. The flies of evening are on their feeble wings; the hum of their course is on the field. What dost thou behold, fair light? But thou dost smile and depart. The waves come with joy around thee: they bathe thy lovely hair. Farewell, thou silent beam! Let the light of Ossian's soul arise!

And it does arise in its strength. I behold my departed friends. Their gathering is on Lora, as in the days of other years. Fingal comes like a watry column of mist; his heroes are around: And see the bards of song, grey-haired Ullin, stately Ryno! Alpin, with the tuneful voice! the soft complaint of Minona! How are ye changed, my friends, since the days of Selma's feast? when we contended, like gales of spring, as they fly along the hill, and bend by turns the feebly-whistling grass.

Minona came forth in her beauty; with downcast look and tearful eye. Her hair flew slowly on the blast, that rushed unfrequent from the hill. The souls of the heroes were sad when she raised the tuneful voice. Often had they seen the groves of Salgar, the dark dwelling of white-bosomed Colma. Colma left alone on the hill with all her voice of song! Salgar promised to come: but the night descended around. Hear the voice of Colma, when she sat alone on the hill!

Colma.

It is night; I am alone, forlorn on the hill of storms. The wind is heard in the mountain. The torrent pours down the rock. No hut receives me from the rain; forlorn on the hill of winds!

Rise moon! from behind thy clouds. Stars of the night arise. Lead me, some light, to the place, where my love rests from the chace alone! his bow near him, unstrung: his dogs panting around him. But here I must sit alone, by the rock of the mossy stream. The stream and the wind roar aloud. I hear not the voice of my love! Why delays my Salgar, why the chief of the hill, his promise? Here is the rock, and here the tree! here is the roaring stream! Thou didst promise with night to be here. Ah! whither is my Salgar gone? With thee I would fly, from my father; with thee from my brother of pride. Our race have long been foes; we are not foes, O Salgar!

Cease a little while, O wind! stream, be thou silent a while! let my voice be heard around. Let my wanderer hear me! Salgar! it is Colma who calls. Here is the tree, and the rock. Salgar, my love! I am here. Why delayest thou thy coming? Lo! the calm moon comes forth. The flood is bright in the vale. The rocks are grey on the steep. I see him not on the brow. His dogs come not before him, with tidings of his near approach. Here I must sit alone!

Who lies on the heath beside me? Are they my love and my brother? Speak to me, O my friends! To Colma they give no reply. Speak to me: I am alone. My soul is tormented with fears! Ah! they are dead! Their swords are red from the fight. O my brother! my brother! why hast thou slain my Salgar? why, O Salgar! hast thou slain my brother? Dear were ye both to me! what shall I say in your praise? Thou wert fair on the hill among thousands! he was terrible in fight. Speak to me; hear my voice; hear me, sons of my love! They are silent; silent for ever! Cold, cold, are their breast of clay! Oh! from the rock on the hill; from the top of the windy steep, speak, ye ghosts of the dead! speak, I will not be afraid! Whither are ye gone to rest? In what cave of the hill shall I find the departed? No feeble voice is on the gale: no answer half-drowned in the storm!

I sit in my grief! I wait for morning in my tears! Rear the tomb, ye friends of the dead. Close it not till Colma come. My life flies away like a dream: why should I stay behind? Here I shall rest with my friends, by the stream of the sounding rock. When night comes on the hill; when the loud winds arise; my ghost shall stand in the blast, and mourn the death of my friends. The hunter shall hear from his booth. He shall fear but love my voice! For sweet shall my voice be for my friends: pleasant were her friends to Colma!

Such was thy song, Minona, softly-blushing daughter of Torman. Our tears descended for Colma, and our souls were sad! Ullin came with his harp; he gave the song to Alpin. The voice of Alpin was pleasant: the soul of Ryno was a beam of fire! But they had rested in the narrow house: their voice had ceased in Selma. Ullin had returned, one day, from the chace, before the heroes fell. He heard their strife on the hill; their song was soft but sad! They mourned the fall of Morar, first of mortal men! His soul was like the soul of Fingal; his sword like the sword of Oscar. But he fell, and his father mourned: his sister's eyes were full of tears. Minona's eyes were full of tears, the sister of car-borne Morar. She retired from the song of Ullin, like the moon in the west, when she foresees the shower, and hides her fair head in a cloud. I touched the harp, with Ullin; the song of mourning rose!

Ryno.

The wind and the rain are past: calm is the noon of day. The clouds are divided in heaven. Over the green hill flies the inconstant sun. Red through the stony vale comes down the stream of the hill. Sweet are thy murmurs, O stream! but more sweet is the voice I hear. It is the voice of Alpin, the son of song, mourning for the dead! Bent is his head of age; red his tearful eye. Alpin, thou son of song, why alone on the silent hill? why complainest thou, as a blast in the wood; as a wave on the lonely shore?

Alpin.

My tears, O Ryno! are for the dead; my voice for those that have passed away. Tall thou art on the hill; fair among the sons of the vale. But thou shalt fall like Morar; the mourner shall sit on thy tomb. The hills shall know thee no more; thy bow shall lie in the hall, unstrung!

Thou were swift, O Morar! as a roe on the desert; terrible as a meteor of fire. Thy wrath was as the storm. Thy sword in battle, as lightning in the field. Thy voice was a stream after rain; like thunder on distant hills. Many fell by thy arm; they were consumed in the flames of thy wrath. But when thou didst return from war, how peaceful was thy brow! Thy face was like the sun after rain; like the moon in the silence of night; calm as the breast of the lake when the loud wind is laid.

Narrow is thy dwelling now! dark the place of thine abode! With three steps I compass thy grave, O thou who was so great before! Four stones, with their heads of moss, are the only memorial of thee. A tree with scarce a leaf, long grass, which whistles in the wind, mark to the hunter's eye the grave of mighty Morar. Morar! thou art low indeed. Thou hast no mother to mourn thee: no maid with her tears of love. Dead is she that brought thee forth. Fallen is the daughter of Morglan.

Who on his staff is this? who is this, whose head is white with age? whose eyes are red with tears? who quakes at every step? It is thy father, O Morar! the father of no son but thee. He heard of thy fame in war; he heard of foes dispersed. He heard of Morar's renown; why did he not hear of his wound? Weep, thou father of Morar! weep; but thy son heareth thee not. Deep is the sleep of the dead; low their pillow of dust. No more shall he hear thy voice; no more awake at thy call. When shall it be morn in the grave, to bid the slumberer awake? Farewell, thou bravest of men! thou conqueror in the field! but the field shall see thee no more; nor the dark wood be lightened with the splendour of thy steel. Thou hast left no son. The song shall preserve thy name. Future times shall hear of thee; they shall hear of the fallen Morar!

The grief of all arose, but most the bursting sigh of Armin. He remembers the death of his son, who fell in the days of his youth. Carmor was near the hero, the chief of the echoing Galmal. Why burst the sigh of Armin, he said? Is there a cause to mourn? The song comes, with its music, to melt and please the soul. It is like soft mist, that, rising from a lake, pours on the silent vale; the green flowers are filled with dew; but the sun returns in his strength, and the mist is gone. Why art thou sad, O Armin, chief of sea-surrounded Gorma!

Sad I am! nor small is my cause of woe! Carmor, thou hast lost no son; thou hast lost no daughter of beauty. Colgar the valiant lives; and Annira, fairest maid. The boughs of thy house ascend, O Carmor! but Armin is the last of his race. Dark is thy bed, O Daura! deep thy sleep in the tomb! When shalt thou awake with thy songs? with all thy voice of music?

Arise, winds of autumn, arise; blow along the heath! streams of the mountains roar! roar tempests, in the groves of my oaks! walk through broken clouds, O moon! show thy pale face at intervals! bring to my mind the night, when all my children fell; when Arindal the mighty fell; when Daura the lovely failed! Daura, my daughter! thou wert fair; fair as the moon on Fura; white as the driven snow; sweet as the breathing gale. Arindal, thy bow was strong. Thy spear was swift in the field. Thy look was like mist on the wave: thy shield a red cloud in a storm. Armor, renowned in war, came, and sought Daura's love. He was not long refused: fair was the hope of their friends!

Erath, son of Odgal, repined: his brother had been slain by Armor. He came disguised like a son of the sea: fair was his skiff on the wave; white his locks of age; calm his serious brow. Fairest of women, he said, lovely daughter of Armin! a rock, not distant in the sea bears a tree on its side; red shines the fruit afar. There Armor waits for Daura. I come to carry his love! She went; she called on Armor. Nought answered but the son of the rock, Armor, my love! my love! why tormentest thou me with fear? hear, son of Armor, hear: it is Daura who calleth thee! Erath the traitor fled laughing to the land. She lifted up her voice; she called for her brother and her father. Arindal! Armin! none to relieve your Daura!

Her voice came over the sea. Arindal, my son, descended from the hill; rough in the spoils of the chace. His arrows rattled by his side; his bow was in his hand: five dark grey dogs attend his steps. He saw fierce Erath on the shore: he seized and bound him to an oak. Thick wind the thongs of the hide around his limbs; he

114

loads the wind with his groans. Arindal ascends the deep in his boat, to bring Daura to land. Armor came in his wrath, and let fly the grey feathered shaft. It sung; it sunk in thy heart, O Arindal my son! for Erath the traitor thou diedst. The oar is stopped at once: he panted on the rock, and expired. What is thy grief, O Daura, when round thy feet is poured thy brother's blood! The boat is broken in twain. Armor plunges into the sea, to rescue his Daura or die. Sudden a blast from the hill came over the waves. He sunk and he rose no more.

Alone, on the sea-beat rock, my daughter was heard to complain. Frequent and loud were her cries. What could her father do? All night I stood on the shore. I saw her by the faint beam of the moon. All night I heard her cries. Loud was the wind; the rain beat hard on the hill. Before morning appeared, her voice was weak. It died away, like the evening breeze among the grass of the rocks. Spent with grief, she expired; and left thee, Armin, alone. Gone is my strength in war! fallen my pride among women! When the storms aloft arise; when the north lifts the wave on high; I sit by the sounding shore, and look on the fatal rock. Often by the setting moon, I see the ghosts of my children. Half-viewless, they walk in mournful conference together. Will none of you speak in pity? They do not regard their father. I am sad, O Carmor; nor small is my cause of woe!

Such were the words of the bards in the days of song; when the king heard the music of harps, the tales of other times! The chiefs gathered from all their hills, and heard the lovely sound. They praised the voice of Cona! the first among a thousand bards! But age is now on my tongue; my soul has failed! I hear, at times, the ghosts of bards, and learn their pleasant song. But memory fails on my mind. I hear the call of years! They say, as they pass along, why does Ossian sing? Soon shall he lie in the narrow house, and no bard shall raise his fame! Roll on, ye dark-brown years; ye bring no joy on your course! Let the tomb open to Ossian; for his strength has failed. The sons of song are gone to rest. My voice remains, like a blast, that roars, lonely, on a sea-surrounded rock, after the winds are laid. The dark moss whistles there; the distant mariner sees the waving-trees.

The Six Bards

FIRST BARD
Night is dull and dark,
The clouds rest on the hills;
No star with twinkling beam,
No moon looks from the skies.
I hear the blast in the wood,
But distant and dull I hear it.
The stream of the valley murmurs,
Low is its murmur too.
From the tree at the grave of the dead,
The lonely screech-owl groans. 10
I see a dim form on the plain,
'Tis a ghost! it fades, it flies;
Some dead shall pass this way.
From the lowly hut of the hill
The distant dog is howling;
The stag lies by the mountain-well,
The hind is at his side;
She hears the wind in his horns,
She starts, but lies again.
The roe is in the cleft of the rock: 20
The heath-cock's head beneath his wing.
No beast, no bird is abroad,
But the owl, and the howling fox;
She on the leafless tree,
He on the cloudy hill.
Dark, panting, trembling, sad,
The traveller has lost his way;
Through shrubs, through thorns he goes,
Beside the gurgling rills;
He fears the rock and the pool, 30
He fears the ghost of the night.
The old tree groans to the blast;
The falling branch resounds.
The wind drives the clung thorn

Along the sighing grass;
He shakes amid the night.
Dark, dusty, howling, is night,
Cloudy, windy, and full of ghosts;
The dead are abroad; my friends
Receive me from the night.   40

SECOND BARD
The wind is up on the mountain;
The shower of the hill descends.
Woods groan, and windows clap;
The growing river roars:
The traveller attempts the ford,
He falls, he shrieks, he dies.
The storm drives the horse from the hill,
The goat and the lowing cow;
They tremble as drives the shower,
And look for a shade of the stall.   10
The hunter starts from sleep in his lone hut,
And wakes the fire decay'd;
His wet dogs smoke around him:
He stops the chinks with heath.
Loud roar two mountain streams,
Which meet beside his booth.
Sad on the side of the hill
The wandering shepherd sits.
The tree resounds above him.
The stream roars down the rock.   20
He waits the rising moon
To lead him to his home.
Ghosts ride on the storm to-night.
Sweet is their voice between the gusts of wind,
Their songs are of other worlds.
    The rain is past. The dry winds blow.
Streams roar and windows clap;
Cold drops fall from the roof.

117

I see the starry sky. –
But the shower gathers again. 30
Dark, dark is the western sky!
Night is stormy, dismal, dark;
Receive me, my friends, from the night.

+ (remarkably like the cadences of "Ossian")

✗ *The Hunter*

II
In Donald's eye now fades the blissful scenes:
The rough brow'd rocks, the sloping hills and plains,
Delight no more; no chace, no winged fowl,
No goat, no cattle, cheer the troubled soul;
The hut is hateful, and the fields of corn
Contract their bounds, and promise no return.
All is one blank – O envy'd, envy'd state,
The hunter cries, of all the happy great!
While press'd in poverty's hard iron hand,
I force poor sustenance from barren land, 10
Remote from life, and curs'd by fate unkind,
To struggle on the hill with northern wind,
Secure, in stately halls, the feast they ply,
And swim through life in deluges of joy.
The hut, the heathy wild, the barren fold,
The rattling hail, the north-descended cold,
Is all my portion – all a swain can boast,
Still 'twixt vicissitude's rough billows toss'd.
O partial Heavens! O Providence unkind!
Mine is the well-strung arm, the feeling mind; 20
Yet scarce can wade through miseries of life,
Combat with care, with care in endless strife.
O why, ye Powers, not bless me with a mind
To all the blasts of poverty resigned,

Or bless me greatly with the affluent store,
Nor doom the hapless hunter to be poor?

*

A hill there is, which forms a sable wall
Through all the north, and men it Grampus call.
Here lean-cheek'd Barrenness terrific strides;
A tattered robe waves round her iron sides;
Two baleful eyes roll in her iron face;
Her meagre hand supports a pile of grass;   60
Her bare white skull no decent covering shews;
Eternal tempests rattle on her brows;
Lank-sided Want, and pale-eyed Poverty,
And sharp-tooth'd Famine, still around her fly;
Health-gotten Hunger, want-descended Pain,
Vein-numbing Cold – are all her gloomy train.
The hunter view'd; a shiv'ring tremour ran
Through every vein, and vanquished all the man:...

III

The king arose, his grateful visage shook,
Then stretched his sceptre, and commanding spoke.   10
    Ye chiefs, ye heroes, ye professed foes
Of hateful slavery and th'aspiring Rose,
If on the iron field, incased in arms,
Ye taught your foes that liberty had charms;
If, dauntless chiefs! ye bore of generous toil,
And met with death to save a barren soil;
Now, now, O! generous lend the timely aid,
And break the storm that threatens Scotia's head.
This to our mother we, her children, owe;
Our country's enemy is still our foe.   20
Bleak Desolation, on her lonely wings,
The foe through all the south terrific brings:
And now, nocturnal, on the yellow sand,

119

In sable walls the embattled English stand
In close array. To-morrow they prepare
To hurl against our walls the stormy war.
Rise, Caledonian chiefs! ye heroes, rise!
Your bleeding country for your succour cries.
Thus in the iron field a father falls,
And grasping his dear son, incessant calls,　　　　　30
Revenge, my son, revenge my death! he cries.
The son obeys – revenges, or he dies.

IV

In dazzling arms the chiefs terrific shine,
Glide through the ranks, and form the lengthening line.　　30
While from the embattled foe a hero strode;
A coat of mail hangs from his shoulders broad;
On his high towering head terrific waved
A crested helmet that the sabre braved.
On his left hand he bears a spacious shield,
Glittering with iron terrour o'er the field;
And in his right he waves the shining blade.
He greatly stood – and thus provoking said:
Ye Scots, ye nation full of fraud and guile!
Ye mean descendants of a barren soil!　　　　　40
Let one advance (the bravest, I demand),
And fall a victim to my conquering hand;
Forget your fears, your wonted fears controul,
Let fate enlarge the ever little soul.
　　He said; and rage, in tickling poison, ran
Through every soul, and stung each generous man.
The Hunter heard; rage sparkled from his eyes,
And from his inmost soul the hero sighs;
And thus indignant spoke: – Ah! glory gone!
Ah! ancient virtue now for ever flown!　　　　　50
What blessed corner does the godhead rest?
No more you swell the generous Scottish breast,
When thus, O Scotland! Saxons dare deride

Thy steel-clad warriors, ranged side by side –
I can no more – my panting vitals swell;
I'll give thee glory, or thy soul to hell.
　　Then towards the foe the youth indignant moved:
Fear trembles, en'mies praise, and envy loved.
He strides along the men-environed ground;
His rattling arms emit an iron sound:　　　　　　　　　60
The Saxon saw, advanced, nor looked behind,
Fate hurried on, and courage steel'd his mind.
Bright in effulgent arms the youths appeared;
Each o'er the plain a steely column reared:
They rush together; clashing arms afar
Reflect the horrours of the dismal war.
Awful the blades wave gleaming in the sky,
And from the crashing steel the sparkles fly.
They fight, and, wearied, cease, and fight again;
Their feet bake dust with blood upon the plain.　　　　70
Death undetermined points to each his stings,
And conquest flutters round on dubious wings.
The hill-born youth reminds, with anxious care,
What vaunts the foul-mouth'd Saxon breath'd on air;
His country's love the youthful hero warms,
And vengeance strung his almost wearied arms.
Upraised aloft, the light reflexive blade
Sings through the air, and cleaves the Saxon's head.
The broken skull, and shiver'd helmet, strew'd
The sandy plain, that reeks with human blood.　　　　80
He gasping falls, and shakes the thundering ground,
And, dying, toss'd his quivering limbs around.

*

O! would to Heaven that thus each Saxon lay;
Then late posterity would bless this day,
The Hunter cries: Nor should it be forgot,
That Steuart's sceptered, and that Donald fought.
But ah! how fading is a mighty name,　　　　　　　165

And but a moment sounds the trump of fame!
Forgot the conqueror and the vanquished die;
No little deeds claim immortality.

On the Death of Marshal Keith

Sad from his native home the chief withdrew;
But kindled Scotia's glory as he flew;   40
On far Iberia built his country's fame,
And distant Russia heard his country's name.
Turks stood aghast, as o'er the fields of war,
He ruled the storm, and urged the martial car.
They asked their chiefs, what state the hero raised;
And Albion on the Hellespont was praised.
   But chiefs, as relics of a dying race,
The Keiths command, in woe, the foremost place;
A name for ages through the world revered,
By Scotia loved, by all her en'mies feared;   50
Now falling, dying, lost to all but fame,
And only living in the hero's name.
   See! the proud halls they once possessed, decayed,
The spiral tow'rs depend the lofty head;
Wild ivy creeps along the mould'ring walls,
And with each gust of wind a fragment falls;
While birds obscene at noon of night deplore,
Where mighty heroes kept the watch before.
   On Mem'ry's tablet mankind soon decay,
On Time's swift stream their glory slides away;   60
But present in the voice of deathless Fame,
Keith lives, eternal, in his glorious name:
While ages far remote his actions show;
And mark with them the way their chiefs should go;
While sires unto their wond'ring offspring tell,
Keith lived in glory, and in glory fell.

✕ *The Monument*

In vain we toil for lasting fame,
Or give to other times our name;
The bust itself shall soon be gone,
The figure moulder from the stone;
The plaintive strain, the moving lay,
Like those they mourn, at last decay:
My name a surer way shall live,
A surer way, my fair can give:
In her dear mem'ry let me live alone;
When NISA dies, I wish not to be known.

Edward Young

Edward Young was born at Upham in Hampshire in 1683, the son of a distinguished clergyman. He was educated at Winchester College, then New College and Corpus Christi at Oxford; and went on to receive a fellowship in law at All Souls. A Victorian editor commented primly of his university days that his conduct 'did not hold out much promise of the virtues that adorned and dignified the remainder of his life'.[1] His first substantial piece, *The Last Day*, a robustly uninhibited apocalyptic vision, appeared in 1713; followed by *The Force of Religion*, a lacklustre account of the final days of Lady Jane Grey in 1714; and *A Paraphrase on Part of the Book of Job* in 1719, notable chiefly for God's extensive familiarity with contemporary meteorology. In the same year Young's first tragedy, *Busiris*, was performed to considerable acclaim. In 1717, he had tutored Philip, Duke of Wharton, and subsequently attached himself to the wayward political fortunes of this brilliant profligate, Jacobin, and one-time president of the Hell-Fire club. The rewards could be considerable: in 1721, his fulsome dedication of his second tragedy, *The Revenge*, was repaid with a gift of £2000; and the series of seven verse satires, published between 1725 and 1728, entitled *The Love of Fame, the Universal Passion*, considered by Johnson to be 'a very great performance',[2] reputedly earnt him £3000.

The final disgrace of Wharton in 1726 removed both Young's hopes of a political career and his chief source of patronage, and he was belatedly ordained the following year, at the age of forty-four. He received the rectorship of Welwyn three years later, but no further ecclesiastical preferment, despite his initial promotion to royal chaplain, literary fame, and indefatigable place-seeking. His literary activity continued throughout his involuntary retirement: a third tragedy, *The Brothers*, had a benefit performance in 1753; a series of prose satires, *The Centaur not Mysterious* were published in 1754; and his last considerable poem, *Resignation*, appeared in 1762. The major work of his final years, however, is undoubtedly *Conjectures on Original Composition* (1759), an eloquently idealistic polemic on behalf of the powers of innate genius. Young's most celebrated poem, *The Complaint, or Night Thoughts on Life, Death, and Immortality*, was composed between 1742 and 1745. Its enormous length (just under 10,000 lines) is divided into nine sections or nights. The first three are ostensibly laments for his wife, Lady Elizabeth Lee, who had died in 1740, her daughter by a previous marriage (Narcissa) and her son-in-law (Philander); the next five attempt to demonstrate 'the nature, proof, and importance of immortality' in order to convert a young debauchee, Lorenzo; the final night offers an extended galactic tour and culminating vision of apocalypse. *Night Thoughts*, along with James Hervey's *Meditations among the Tombs* and Robert Blair's *The Grave*, established what has become known as the 'Graveyard school' (most famously represented by Gray's 'Elegy written in a Country Churchyard').

The genre's solitary meditations on human mortality have traditionally been seen as an important point of transition towards Romanticism in their unabashed egotism, absence of rhetorical self-restraint, and characteristic alienation. The preface to *Night Thoughts* appears to support this: 'as the occasion for the poem was *real* not *fictitious*: so the method pursued in it, was rather *imposed* by what spontaneously arose in the author's mind on that occasion, than *meditated* or *designed*'. But there is no interest whatsoever in psychological verisimilitude: the processes of mental connection, so nuanced and implicit in Gray and Collins, are here overt and rhetorical. Memory is not personal in the post-Wordsworthian sense of uniquely constitutive, and only belongs uneasily in the Augustinian tradition of religious confession. The poem appears to demand a comprehensive retrospective totting-up, yet despite its sheer bulk, there is virtually no autobiographical content; the few discernible allusions are almost provocatively refutable. (For example, Young's son, once presumed to be the model for Lorenzo, was only eight when the poem was written.)

For the next fifty years, *Night Thoughts* was incessantly republished and translated into twelve languages. Like Macpherson's *Ossian*, the poem acquired a separate momentum in the history of European Romanticism, culminating in André Breton's enthusiastic acclaim in the *Manifeste du Surréalisme* (1924). In 1857, however, Young's English reputation, already waning, was damaged beyond repair by George Eliot's essay, 'Worldliness and Other-Worldliness: the Poet Young'. Much of her criticism depends on a blunt juxtaposition of the imperfections of the life (notably the 'fervent attachment to patrons in general') with the sanctimoniousness of the work, but her central charge of *'radical insincerity as a poetic artist'* has more interesting implications.[3] Young is denounced as 'the type of that deficient human sympathy, that impiety towards the present and visible, which flies for its motives, its sanctities and its religion, to the remote, the vague, and the unknown' (p.387). *Night Thoughts* certainly 'flies' from any such dependence on the 'present and visible' or authenticity founded thereon: the night-time vigil demands that all human relationships be cast off as mere worldly attachments – 'But friends, how mortal! dang'rous the desire' (3:18). Whereas the day-time thoughts exposed to the sensory world are 'impos'd, precarious, broken e'er mature', nocturnal speculations 'uncontroul'd and unimpress'd, the Births/ Of pure Election, arbitrary range' (5:118-21).

Night Thoughts is a supremely undidactic poem, its pretence at ratiocination invariably local and opportunist. We grow to feel that these are only matters of life and death, nothing important: 'Or Life, or Death, is equal; neither weighs' (4:150). The power of nature lies in its subjection of the body to time and hence mortality; Young's poetic voice refuses to concede this dependence. It remains completely disembodied, impossible to situate either spatially or perspectively. Its ascendancy depends neither on the coherence of its arguments nor on the persuasion of an opponent, but on its own tirelessly ingenious self-perpetuation – what Johnson called Young's 'copiousness' and Gray his 'redundancy of thought'.[4]

George Eliot attempts to salvage the 'morbid exaggerations' of the earlier nights psychologically: 'there is already some artificiality even in his grief, and feeling often slides into rhetoric, but through it all we are thrilled with the unmistakeable cry of pain, which makes us tolerant of egoism and hyperbole' (pp.365-6). I would reverse this: though there may be some grief even in Young's artificiality, the pleasure and power of his text lie not in an authenticity momentarily brought on by pressure of bereavement, but in a linguistic exhibitionism pushed to the point of paradoxical selfless-ness. Instead of the Wordsworthian ideal of a 'spontaneous overflow of powerful feelings', there's a rhetoric of overworked surface in the service of hyperbolic declamation, brazen, coarse, almost frivolous in its habitual self-induced histrionics – 'Is it a Stygian vapour in my Blood,/ A cold slow Puddle creeping through my Veins' (5:218-19). It represents an extreme mutation of a Senecan format, aphoristic, ejaculatory, static, self-elaborating: the extreme segmentation of the verse, its over-punctuation, its insistence on the line-unit, are all designed to give the minimum personal inflection. There is no attempt at synthesis, merely mutually exacerbating polarities of feeling. Johnson refers to Young's 'ebullitions', the keeping of liquid at boiling point, the moment of its transformation into gas, and remarks, almost fondly, 'let burlesque try to go beyond him'.[5]

What is most striking in Edmund Burke's classic account of the sublime is his break with any correspondence theory of poetry: if 'a clear idea is a lit-tle idea', the most intense aesthetic experiences necessarily derive from the evocation of infinity, darkness, solitude and terror. It is only a short step from his argument that the 'power of raising sensible images' deprives poetry of a 'considerable part of its energy' to a rhetoric whose 'force' depends on the systematic evacuation of any sensory underpinning what-soever.[6] Thus the language of *Night Thoughts* can be said, in a precise and unpejorative sense, to be vacuous: it flaunts the power of genius 'to reign arbitrarily over its own empire of Chimeras'.[7] 'The grandiloquent man,' as George Eliot says, 'may float away into utter inanity' (pp.366-7). An initial enclosure within the 'contracted Circle' of self and world (9:589) is followed by a vertiginous and open-ended expansion: 'Embryos must we be, till we burst the shell,/ Yon ambient, azure shell, and spring to Life' (1:132-3). But the posited vantage is structural rather than spiritual, somewhere to see from rather than reside in; the immortality from which the 'due-distanced eye' (6:595) derides its previous constraints is an essentially satiric perspec-tive.[8]

In *Night Thoughts*, there is a convergence between the two major strands of Young's development: religious sublimity and satiric epistle. *Love of Fame* follows the classical bipartite structure of first arraigning a specific

vice, then asserting the correspondent virtue. The worldly commentary –
sententious musing interspersed with the occasional sleazy, barbed, or
surreal aside ('Like Cats in air-pumps, to subsist we strive' (5:177)) – works
quite well, but there remains a feeling of listlessness, a certain smugness in
its supposedly shared and self-evident values. *Night Thoughts* expands the
opposition between vice and virtue into a sweeping antithesis between a
wholly unredeemable world and a 'great soul', aged, bereaved, immersed
in silence and darkness, castigating from a 'high point/ Leaving gross
Nature's Sediments behind' (6:251-2). It may be usefully compared to other
forms of post-Augustan satire, particularly that of Charles Churchill. This,
though topical and specific, is similarly bellicose, digressive and
uncumulative. The poet, devoid of any supportive community, is compel-
led to rely on the coercive force of his relentless pugnacity; the measure of
his poetic authority is the spontaneousness of his abuse (or the abusiveness
of his spontaneity). This results in a magnification of both satirist and target
into a kind of declamatory melodrama: there is a kind of no-holds-barred
gusto, almost scurrility, in Young's denunciation of the 'snout of grov'ling
Appetite' (8:615) and the 'coarse Drudgeries, and Sinks of Sense' (7:1213).
There is no common feeling for the body, as in the great Jacobean tirades
against sensuality and mortality; it is a polemic delivered from outside, but
because of that achieves a kind of licensed extremity, the lyricism of utter
estrangement. And though it may be too much to expect that *Night
Thoughts* be restored to the literary canon in its entirety, I hope the selec-
tions here provided will at least allow some appreciation of the challenge
laid down by its *'radical insincerity'*: 'Art thou so moor'd thou canst not dis-
engage?' (2:389).

✕ The Last Day

II
Again the Trumpet's intermitted Sound
Rouls the wide Circuit of Creation round,
An universal Concourse to prepare
Of all that ever breath'd the vital Air,
In some wide Field, which active Whirlwinds sweep,
Drive Cities, Forests, Mountains to the Deep,
To smooth, and Lengthen out the Unbounded Space,
And Spread an Area for all Human Race.   20
    Now Monuments prove faithful to their Trust,
And render back their long-committed Dust,

Now Charnels Rattle; scatter'd Limbs, and all
The various Bones, obsequious to the Call,
Self-mov'd, advance; the Neck perhaps to meet
The distant Head, the distant Legs, the Feet;
Dreadful to View! see thro' the Dusky Sky
Fragments of Bodies in Confusion fly,
To distant Regions journying, there to claim
Deserted Members, and compleat the Frame.   30

*

The Trumpet's Sound each vagrant Mote shall hear,
Or fix'd in Earth, or if afloat in Air,
Obey the Signal, wafted in the Wind,
And not one Sleeping Atom lag behind.
   So swarming Bees, that, on a Summer's Day
In airy Rings, and wild Meanders play,   50
Charm'd with the brazen Sound, their Wand'rings end,
And gently circling on a Bough Descend.

*

Nor Monuments alone, and Burial-Earth,
Labour with Man to this his second Birth;
But where gay Palaces in Pomp arise,
And gilded Theatres invade the Skies,
Nations shall wake, whose unsuspected Bones
Support the Pride of their Luxurious Sons;
The most magnificent, and costly Dome
Is but an upper Chamber to a Tomb,
No Spot on earth but has supply'd a Grave,
And Human Skulls the spatious Ocean pave,   90
All's full of Man, and at this dreadful Turn,
The Swarm shall Issue, and the Hive shall burn.

*

A sudden Blush inflames the waving Sky,
And now the crimson Curtains open fly,   210
Lo! far within, far far above all Height,
Whv're Heav'n's Great Sovereign reigns in Worlds of Light,
Whence Nature He informs, and with one Ray
Shot from his Eye, does all her Works survey,
Creates, supports, confounds! Where Time, and Place,
Matter, and Form, and Fortune, Life and Grace,
Wait humbly at the Footstool of their God,
And move Obedient at his Awful Nod;
Whence he beholds us vagrant Emmets crawl
At random on this Air-suspended Ball,   220
(Speck of Creation!) if He pour one Breath,
The Bubble breaks, and 'tis Eternal Death.

III

That Woe, those Pangs which from the guilty breast,
In these or Words like these, shall be Exprest: –
    'Who burst the Barriers of my peacefull Grave?
Ah! Cruel Death that wou'd no longer Save,
But grudg'd me e'en that narrow, dark Abode,
And cast me out into the Wrath of God;
Where Shreeks, the roaring Flame, the ratling Chain,
And all the Dreadful Eloquence of Pain
Our only Song; Black Fire's Malignant Light,   130
The sole Refreshment of the blasted Sight.

                                    *

Never! where falls the Soul at that dread sound,
Down an abyss how dark, and how profound,
Down, down I still am falling, (Horrid Pain!)
Ten thousand thousand Fathoms still remain,
My plunge but still begun. And this for sin?   160
Could I Offend, if I had never been,
But still encreast the senseless happy Mass,

Flow'd in the stream, or shiver'd in the grass?
'Father of Mercies! why from silent Earth
Didst thou awake, and curse me into Birth?
Tear me from Quiet, ravish me from Night,
And make a thankless Present of thy Light;
Push into Being a Reverse of Thee,
And animate a Clod with Misery?'

*

Deep Anguish! but too late! the hopeless Soul
Bound to the Bottom of the burning Pool,
Tho' loath, and Ever loud blaspheming, owns   210
He's Justly doom'd to pour Eternal Groans;
Enclost with Horrors, and transfixt with Pain,
Rowling in Vengeance, struggling with his Chain,
To talk to fiery Tempests; to implore
The raging Flame to give its Burnings o'er,
To Toss, to Writhe, to Pant beneath his Load
And bear the Weight Of an Offended God.

✕ *Love of Fame: The Universal Passion*

V
Britannia's daughters, much more fair than nice,
Too fond of Admiration, lose their price;
Worn in the publick eye, give cheap delight
To throngs, and tarnish to the sated sight.
As unreserv'd and beauteous, as the Sun,
Thro' every Sign of Vanity they run;   20
Assemblies, parks, coarse feasts in city-halls,
Lectures and trials, plays, committees, balls,
Wells, Bedlams, executions, Smith-field scenes,
And fortune-tellers' caves, and lyon's dens,

Taverns, Exchanges, Bridewells, drawing-rooms,
Instalments, pillories, coronations, tombs,
Tumblers, and funerals, puppet-shows, reviews,
Sales, races, rabbets, and, (still stranger!) pews.

*

A dearth of words, a Woman need not fear,
But 'tis a task indeed to learn – to hear.
In that the skill of conversation lyes,
That shows, or makes you both polite, and wise.   60
   Zantippe crys, 'let Nymphs who nought can say,
Be lost in silence, and resign the day:
And let the guilty wife her guilt confess
By tame behaviour, and a soft address.'
Thro' virtue, she refuses to comply
With all the dictates of humanity;
Thro' wisdom she refuses to submit
To wisdom's rules, and raves to prove her wit:
Then, her unblemisht honour to maintain,
Rejects her husband's kindness with disdain.   70
But if, by chance, an ill-adapted word
Drops from the lip of her unwary Lord,
Her darling China in a whirlwind sent
Just intimates the Lady's discontent.
   Wine may indeed excite the meekest dame,
But keen Zantippe scorning borrow'd flame,
Can vent her thunders, and her lightnings play,
O'er cooling gruel, and composing tea.
Nor rests by night, but, more sincere than nice,
She shakes the curtains with her kind advice.   80
Doubly like Eccho, sound is her delight,
And the last word is her eternal right.
Is 't not enough plagues, wars, and famines rise
To lash our crimes, but must our wives be wise?

*

Sempronia lik'd her man, and well she might,
The youth in person, and in parts was bright;
Possest of every virtue, grace, and art,
That claims just empire o'er the female heart.
He met her passion, all her sighs return'd,
And in full rage of youthful ardour burn'd.   160
Large his possessions, and beyond her own;
Their bliss the theme, and envy of the town.
The day was fix'd; when with one acre more
In stept deform'd, debaucht, diseas'd threescore.
The fatal sequel, I thro' shame forbear.
Of pride, and av'rice who can cure the Fair?
    Man's rich with little were his judgement true,
Nature is frugal, and her wants are few;
Those few wants answer'd bring sincere delights,
But fools create themselves new appetites.   170
Fancy, and Pride seek things at vast expence,
Which relish not to reason, nor to sense.
When surfeit, or unthankfulness destroys,
In nature's narrow sphere, our solid joys,
In fancy's airy land of noise, and show,
Where nought but dreams, no real pleasures grow,
Like Cats in air-pumps, to subsist we strive
On joys too thin to keep the soul alive.

VI
  Flavia is constant to her old Gallant,
And generously supports him in his want.
But marriage is a fetter, is a snare,
A hell, no Lady so polite can bear.
She's faithful, she's observant, and with pains
Her angel-brood of bastards she maintains.
Nor least advantage has the Fair to plead,
But that of guilt, above the marriage-bed.   70
    Amasia hates a prude, and scorns restraint;
Whate'er she is, she'll not appear a saint.

Her soul superior flies formality,
So gay her air, her conduct is so free,
Some might suspect the nymph not over-good –
Nor wou'd they be mistaken, if they shou'd.
   Unmarry'd Abra puts on formal airs;
Her cushion's thread-bare with her constant prayers.
Her only grief is, that she cannot be
At once engaged in prayer and charity.   80
And this, to do her justice, must be said,
'Who wou'd not think that Abra was a maid?'
   Some Ladies are too beauteous to be wed,
For where's the man that's worthy of their bed?
If no disease reduce her pride before,
Lavinia will be ravisht at threescore.
Then she submits to venture in the dark;
And nothing, now, is wanting – but her spark.

*

Julia's a manager; she's born for rule,
And knows her wiser husband is a fool;   180
Assemblies holds, and spins the subtle thread
That guides the lover to the fair one's bed;
For difficult amours can smooth the way,
And tender letters dictate, or convey.
But if depriv'd of such important cares,
Her wisdom condescends to less affairs.
For her own breakfast she'll project a scheme,
Nor take her Tea without a strategem;
Presides o'er trifles with a serious face,
Important by the virtue of grimace.   190
   Ladies supream among amusements reign,
By nature born to sooth, and entertain;
Their prudence in a share of folly lies,
Why will they be so weak, as to be wise?
   Syrena is for ever in extreams,
And with a vengeance she commends, or blames.
Conscious of her discernment, which is good,

She strains too much to make it understood.
Her judgement just, her sentence is too strong;
Because she's right, she's ever in the wrong.   200

   Brunetta's wise in actions great, and rare;
But scorns on trifles to bestow her care.
Thus every hour Brunetta is to blame,
Because the occasion is beneath her aim.
Think nought a trifle, tho' it small appear;
Small sands the mountain, moments make the years,
And trifles life. Your care to trifles give,
Or you may die, before you truly live.

   Go breakfast with Alicea, there you'll see
Simplex munditiis, to the last degree.   210
Unlac'd her stays, her night-gown is unty'd,
And what she has of head-dress is aside.
She drawls her words, and waddles in her pace;
Unwasht her hands, and much besnuff'd her face.
A nail uncut, and head uncomb'd she loves;
And would draw on jack-boots, as soon as gloves.
Gloves by queen Bess's maidens might be mist,
Her blessed eyes ne'er saw a female fist.
Lovers beware! to wound how can she fail
With scarlet finger, and long jetty nail?   220
For Hervey the first wit she cannot be,
Nor cruel Richmond the first toast for thee;
Since full each other station of renown,
Who would not be the greatest Trapes in town?
Women were made to give our eyes delight,
A female sloven is an odious sight.

*

Here might I sing of Memmia's mincing mein,
And all the movements of the soft machine;
How two red lips affected zephyrs blow,
To cool the bohea, and inflame the beau;
While one white finger, and a thumb, conspire
To lift the cup, and make the world admire.

Tea! how I tremble at thy fatal stream?
As Lethe, dreadful to the love of fame.
What devastations on thy banks are seen?
What shades of mighty names which once have been?   350
A Hecatomb of characters supplies
Thy painted altars daily sacrifice.
Hervey, Pearce, Blount, asperst by thee, decay,
As grains of finest sugar melt away,
And recommend thee more to mortal taste;
Scandal's the sweet'ner of a female feast.

*

O Juvenal! for thy severer rage!
To lash the ranker follies of our age.
    Are there, among the females of our isle
Such faults, at which it is a fault to smile?
There are. Vice, once by modest nature chain'd,
And legal ties, expatiates unrestrain'd,
Without thin decency held up to view,
Naked she stalks o'er the law, and gospel too.
Our matrons lead such exemplary lives,
Men sigh in vain, for none, but for their wives;   380
Who marry to be free, to range the more,
And wed one man, to wanton with a score.
Abroad too kind, at home 'tis steadfast hate,
And one eternal tempest of debate.
When foul eruptions from a look most meek?
What thunders bursting from a dimpled cheek?
Their passions bear it with a lofty hand;
But then their reason is at due command.
Is there whom you detest, and seek his life?
Trust no soul with the secret – but his wife.   390
Wives wonder that their conduct I condemn,
And ask, what kindred is a spouse to them?
    What swarms of amorous grandmothers I see?
And Misses, antient in iniquity!

What blasting whispers, and what loud declaiming?
What lying, drinking, bawding, swearing, gaming?
Friendship so cold, such warm incontinence,
Such gripping avarice, such profuse expense,
Such dead devotion, such a zeal for crimes,
Such licens'd ill, such masquerading times,   400
Such venal faith, such misapply'd applause,
Such flatter'd guilt, and such inverted laws,
Such dissolution thro' the whole I find,
'Tis not a world, but Chaos of Mankind.

(cf Pope's "Epistle on the
characters of Women" for
comparison.)

October 1745

Some thoughts occasioned by the present juncture

Britain? That Word pronounc'd, is an Alarm:
It warms the Blood, tho' frozen in our Veins;
Awakes the Soul, and sends her to the Field,
Enamour'd of the glorious Face of Death.
Britain? – There's noble magic in the Sound.
O what illustrious Images arise?   120
Embattled, round me, blazes the Pomps of War.
By Sea, by Land, at Home, in Foreign Climes,
What full-blown Laurels, on our Father's Brows?
Ye radiant Trophies! and imperial Spoils!
Ye Scenes! Astonishing to modern Sight!
Let me, at least, enjoy you in a Dream;
Why vanish? Stay, ye Godlike Strangers! stay.
Strangers! – I wrong my Countrymen. They wake;
High beats the Pulse; the noble Pulse of War
Beats to that antient Measure, that Grand March,   130
Which, then, prevail'd, when Britain highest soar'd;
And every Battle pay'd for Heroes slain.
No more our great Forefathers stain our Cheeks
With Blushes; Their Renown, our Shame, no more.

In military Garb, and sudden Arms,
Up starts Old Britain; Crosiers are laid by;
Trade wields the Sword; and Agriculture leaves
Her half-turn'd Furrow: Other Harvests fire
A noble Avarice; Avarice of Renown!
And Laurels are the Growth of every Field.   140
In distant Courts is our Commotion felt;
And less like Gods, fit Monarchs on their Thrones.
What Arm can want, or Sinews, or Success,
Which, lifted from an honest Heart, descends,
With all the Weight of British Wrath, to cleave
The Papal Mitre, or the Gallic Chain,
At every Stroke; and save a sinking Land?
Or Death, or Victory, must be resolved;
To dream of Mercy, O how Tame! how Mad!
Where, o'er black Deeds, the Crucifix display'd,   150
Fools think Heaven purchas'd by the Blood they shed;
By giving, not supporting, Pains and Death?
Nor simple Death! When They, the greatest Saints,
Who must subdue all Tenderness of Heart;
Students in Tortures! When, in Zeal to Him,
Whose darling Title is the Prince of Peace;
The Best turn ruthless Butchers, for our Sakes;
To save us in a World, they Recommend,
And yet Forbear; Themselves with Earth content;
And chiefly Those, who Rome's first Honours wear,   160
Whose Name, from Jesus; and whose Arts, from Hell.   *the young*
And shall a Pope-bred Princeling crawl ashore, ——   *Pretender*
Replete with Venom, Guiltless of a Sting,
And whistle Cut-throats, with these Swords, that scrap'd
Their barren Rocks, for wretched Sustenance,
To cut his Passage to the British Throne?
One, that has suck'd in Malice with his Milk,
Malice to Britain, Liberty, and Truth?
Less savage was his Brother-Robber's Nurse,
The howling Nurse of plundering Romulus   170
Ere yet, far worse than Pagan harbour'd there.

137

The Complaint: or, Night Thoughts on Life, Death, and Immortality

NIGHT THE FIRST

Tir'd nature's sweet Restorer, balmy Sleep!
He, like the World, his ready visit pays,
Where Fortune smiles; the wretched he forsakes:
Swift on his downy pinion flies from Woe,
And lights on Lids unsully'd with a Tear.
    From short, (as usual) and disturb'd Repose,
I wake: How happy they who wake no more!
Yet that were vain, if Dreams infest the Grave.
I wake, emerging from a sea of Dreams
Tumultuous; whence my wreck'd, desponding Thought   10
From wave to wave of fancy'd Misery,
At random drove, her helm of Reason lost;
Tho' now restor'd, 'tis only Change of pain,
A bitter change; severer for severe:
The Day too short for my Distress! and Night
Even in the Zenith of her dark Domain,
Is Sun-shine, to the colour of my Fate.
    Night, sable Goddess! from her Ebon throne,
In rayless Majesty, now stretches forth
Her leaden Scepter o'er a slumbering world: 20
Silence, how dead? and Darkness, how profound?
Nor Eye, nor list'ning Ear an object finds;
Creation sleeps. 'Tis, as the general Pulse
Of life stood still, and Nature made a Pause;
An aweful pause! prophetic of her End.
And let her prophecy be soon fulfill'd;
Fate! drop the curtain; I can lose no more.
    Silence, and Darkness! solemn Sisters! Twins
From antient Night, who nurse the tender Thought
To Reason; and on reason build Resolve,   30
(That column of true Majesty in man!)
Assist me: I will thank you in the Grave;
The grave, your Kingdom: There this Frame shall fall

A victim sacred to your dreary shrine:
But what are Ye? Thou, who didst put to flight
Primaeval Silence, when the Morning Stars,
Exulting, shouted o'er the rising Ball;
O thou! whose Word from solid Darkness struck
That spark, the Sun; strike Wisdom from my soul;
My soul which flies to thee, her Trust, her Treasure;   40
As misers to their Gold, while others rest.
    Thro' this Opaque of Nature, and of Soul,
This double Night, transmit one pitying ray,
To lighten, and to chear; O lead my Mind,
(A Mind that fain would wander from its Woe,)
Lead it thro' various scenes of Life and Death,
And from each scene, the noblest Truths inspire:
Nor less inspire my Conduct, than my Song;
Teach my best Reason, Reason; my best Will
Teach Rectitude; and fix my firm Resolve   50
Wisdom to wed, and pay her long Arrear.
Nor let the vial of thy Vengeance pour'd
On this devoted head, be pour'd in vain.
    The Bell strikes One: We take no note of Time,
But from its Loss. To give it then a Tongue,
Is wise in man. As if an Angel spoke,
I feel the solemn Sound. If heard aright,
It is the Knell of my departed Hours;
Where are they? with the years beyond the Flood:
It is the Signal that demands Dispatch;   60
How Much is to be done? my Hopes and Fears
Start up alarm'd, and o'er life's narrow Verge
Look down – on what? a fathomless Abyss;
A dread Eternity! how surely mine!
And can Eternity belong to me,
Poor Pensioner on the bounties of an Hour?
    How poor? how rich? how abject? how august?
How complicate? how wonderful is Man?
How passing wonder He, who made him such?
Who center'd in our make such strange Extremes?   70

139

From different Natures, marvelously mixt,
Connection exquisite of distant Worlds!
Distinguisht Link in Being's endless Chain!
Midway from Nothing to the Deity!
A Beam etherial sully'd, and absorpt!
Tho' sully'd, and dishonour'd, still Divine!
Dim Miniature of Greatness absolute!
An Heir of Glory! a frail Child of Dust!
Helpless Immortal! Insect infinite!
A Worm! a God! I tremble at myself,   80
And in myself am lost! At home a Stranger,
Thought wanders up and down, surpriz'd, aghast,
And wond'ring at her own: How Reason reels?

*

This is the bud of Being, the dim Dawn,
The twilight of our Day; the Vestibule,
Life's Theater as yet is shut, and Death,
Strong Death alone can heave the massy Bar,
This gross impediment of Clay remove,
And make us Embryos of Existence free.
From real life, but little more remote
Is He, not yet a candidate for Light,
The future Embryo, slumbering in his Sire.   130
Embryos we must be, till we burst the Shell,
Yon ambient, azure shell, and spring to Life,
The life of Gods: O Transport! and of Man.
   Yet man, fool man! here burys all his Thoughts;
Inters celestial Hopes without one Sigh:
Prisoner of Earth, and pent beneath the Moon,
Here pinions all his Wishes; wing'd by Heaven
To fly at Infinite; and reach it there,
Where Seraphs gather Immortality,
On life's fair Tree, fast by the throne of God: 140

*

Where falls this Censure? It o'erwhelms myself.
How was my Heart incrusted by the World?
O how self-fetter'd was my groveling Soul?
How, like a Worm, was I wrapt round and round
In silken thought, which reptile Fancy spun,
Till darken'd Reason lay quite clouded o'er
With soft conceit, of endless Comfort here,   160
Nor yet put forth her Wings to reach the skies?

*

O ye blest scenes of permanent Delight!   180
Full, above measure! lasting, beyond bound!
A Perpetuity of Bliss, is Bliss.
Could you, so rich in rapture, fear an End,
That ghastly Thought would drink up all your Joy,
And quite unparadise the realms of Light.
Safe are you lodg'd above these rowling Spheres;
The baleful influence of whose giddy Dance,
Sheds sad Vicissitude on all beneath.
Here teems with Revolutions every Hour.
And rarely for the better; or the best,   190
More mortal than the common births of Fate.
Each Moment has its Sickle, emulous
Of Time's enormous Scythe, whose ample Sweep
Strikes Empires from the root; each Moment plays
His little Weapon in the narrower sphere
Of sweet domestic Comfort, and cuts down
The fairest bloom of sublunary Bliss.
   Bliss! sublunary Bliss! proud words! and vain:
Implicit Treason to divine Decree!
A bold Invasion of the rights of Heaven!   200
I clasp'd the Phantoms, and I found them Air.
O had I weigh'd it e'er my fond Embrace!
What darts of Agony had miss'd my heart?
Death! Great Proprietor of all! 'Tis thine
To tread out Empire, and to quench the Stars;
The Sun himself by thy permission shines,

141

And, one day, thou shalt pluck him from his sphere.
Amid such mighty Plunder, why exhaust
Thy partial Quiver on a Mark so mean?
Why, thy peculiar rancor wreck'd on me?   210
Insatiate Archer! could not One suffice?
Thy shaft flew thrice, and thrice my Peace was slain;
And thrice, e'er thrice yon Moon had fill'd her Horn:
O Cynthia! why so pale? Dost thou lament
Thy wretched Neighbour? Grieve, to see thy Wheel
Of ceaseless change outwhirl'd in human Life?
How wanes my borrow'd bliss! from Fortune's smile,
Precarious Courtesy! not Virtue's sure,
Self-given, solar, ray of sound Delight.

In every vary'd Posture, Place, and Hour,   220
How widow'd every Thought of every Joy!
Thought, busy Thought! too busy for my Peace,
Thro' the dark Postern of Time long elaps'd,
Led softly, by the stillness of the Night,
Led, like a Murderer, (and such it proves!)
Strays, wretched Rover! o'er the pleasing Past,
In quest of wretchedness perversely strays;
And finds all Desart now; and meets the Ghosts
Of my departed Joys; a numerous Train!

*

Mine dy'd with thee, Philander! thy last Sigh
Dissolv'd the charm; the disenchanted Earth
Lost all her Lustre; where, her glittering Towers?
Her golden Mountains, where? all darken'd down
To naked Waste; a dreary Vale of Tears;
The great Magician's dead! Thou poor, pale Piece
Of out-cast earth, in Darkness! what a Change   350
From yesterday! Thy darling Hope so near,
(Long-labour'd Prize!) O how Ambition flush'd
Thy glowing cheek? Ambition truly great,
Of virtuous Praise: Death's subtle seed within,
(Sly, treacherous Miner!) working in the Dark,

Smil'd at thy well-concerted scheme, and beckon'd
The Worm to riot on that Rose so red,
Unfaded e'er it fell; one moment's Prey!
    Man's Foresight is conditionally wise;
Lorenzo! Wisdom into Folly turns   360
Oft, the first instant, its Idea fair
To labouring Thought is born. How dim our eye!
The present Moment terminates our sight;
Clouds, thick as those on Doomsday, drown the next;
We penetrate, we prophesy in vain.
Time is dealt out by Particles; and each,
E'er mingled with the streaming sands of Life,
By Fate's inviolable oath is sworn
Deep silence, 'Where Eternity begins.'
    By Nature's Law, what may be, may be now;   370
There's no Prerogative in human Hours:
In human hearts what bolder Thought can rise,
Than man's Presumption on To-morrow's dawn?
Where is To-morrow? In another world.

                         *

Be wise to day, 'tis madness to defer;
Next day the fatal Precedent will plead;   390
Thus on, till Wisdom is push'd out of life:
Procrastination is the Thief of Time,
Year after year it steals, till all are fled,
And to the mercies of a Moment leaves
The vast Concerns of an Eternal scene.
If not so frequent, would not this be strange?
That, 'tis so frequent, This, is stranger still.
    Of Man's miraculous Mistakes, this bears
The Palm, 'That all Men are about to live'.
For ever on the Brink of being born: 400
All pay themselves the compliment to think
They, one day, shall not drivel; and their Pride
On this Reversion takes up ready Praise;
At least, their own; their future selves applauds;

                        143

How excellent that Life they ne'er will lead?
Time lodg'd in their own hands is Folly's Vails;
That lodg'd in Fate's, to Wisdom they consign;
The thing they can't but purpose, they postpone;
'Tis not in Folly, not to scorn a Fool;
And scarce in human Wisdom to do more: 410
All Promise is poor dilatory man,
And that thro' every Stage: When young, indeed,
In full content, we sometimes nobly rest,
Unanxious for ourselves; and only wish,
As duteous sons, our Fathers were more Wise:
At thirty man suspects himself a Fool;
Knows it at forty, and reforms his Plan;
At fifty chides his infamous Delay,
Pushes his prudent Purpose to Resolve;
In all the magnaminity of Thought   420
Resolves; and re-resolves; then dies the same.
    And why? Because he thinks himself Immortal.
All men think all men Mortal, but themselves...

NIGHT THE SECOND
Where is that Thrift, that Avarice of Time,
(O glorious Avarice!) thought of Death inspires,
As rumour'd robberies endear our Gold?
O Time! than Gold more sacred; more a Load
Than Lead, to Fools; and Fools reputed Wise.
What Moment granted Man without account?   30
What Years are squander'd, Wisdom's debt unpaid?
Our Wealth in Days all due to that discharge.
Haste, haste, He lies in wait, He's at the door,
Insidious Death! should his strong hand arrest,
No Composition sets the Prisoner free.
Eternity's inexorable chain
Fast binds; and Vengeance claims the full Arrear.

*

144

Ah! how unjust to Nature, and Himself,
Is thoughtless, thankless, inconsistent Man?
Like Children babling nonsense in their sports
We censure Nature for a Span too short;
That Span too short, we tax as tedious too,
Torture Invention, all Expedients tire,
To lash the ling'ring moments into speed;
And whirl us (happy riddance!) from ourselves.
Art, brainless Art! our furious Charioteer   120
(For Nature's voice unstifled would recall)
Drives, headlong down towards the precipice of Death;
Death, most our Dread; Death thus more Dreadful made.
O what a Riddle of absurdity?
Leisure is pain; takes off our Chariot-wheels;
How heavily we drag the Load of Life?
Blest Leisure is our Curse, like that of Cain
It makes us wander; wander earth around
To fly that Tyrant, Thought. As Atlas groan'd
The world beneath, we groan beneath an Hour.   130
We cry for Mercy to the next Amusement;
The next Amusement mortgages our fields;
Slight inconvenience! Prisons hardly frown,
From hateful Time, if Prisons set us free.
Yet when Death kindly tenders us Relief,
We call him cruel; Years to Moments shrink,
Ages to Years: The Telescope is turn'd:
To man's false opticks (from his Folly false)
Time, in advance, behind him hides his Wings,
And seems to creep, decrepit with his Age;   140
Behold him, when past by; what then is seen
But his broad Pinions swifter than the winds?
And all Mankind, in Contradiction strong,
Ruefull, aghast! cry out on his Career.

*

All-sensual Man, because untouch'd, unseen,
He looks on Time, as nothing. Nothing else

145

Is truly Man's; tis Fortune's. – Time's a God.
Hast Thou ne'er heard of Time's Omnipotence;
For, or against, what Wonders can He do?
And will: to stand blank Neuter He disdains.
Not on those terms was Time, (Heaven's Stranger!) sent
On his important Embassy to Man.
Lorenzo! no: On the long-destin'd Hour,   200
From everlasting Ages growing ripe,
That memorable Hour of wond'rous Birth,
When the Dread Sire, on Emanation bent,
And big with Nature, rising in his might,
Call'd forth Creation, (for then Time was born),
By Godhead streaming thro' a thousand Worlds,
Not on those Terms, from the great days of Heaven,
From old Eternity's mysterious Orb,
Was Time cut off, and cast beneath the Skies;
The Skies, which watch him in his new abode,   210
Measuring his Motions by revolving Spheres;
That Horologe Machinery Divine.
Hours, Days, and Months, and Years, his Children, play,
Like numerous wings around him, as he flies:
Or, rather, as unequal Plumes, they shape
His ample Pinions, swift as darted Flame,
To gain his goal, to reach his ancient Rest,
And join anew Eternity his Sire;
In his Immutability to nest,
When Worlds, that count his Circles now, unhing'd,   220
(Fate the loud signal sounding) headlong rush
To timeless Night, and Chaos, whence they rose.

*

  O Treacherous Conscience! when she seems to sleep,
On Rose and Myrtle, lull'd with Syren Song;
While she seems, nodding o'er her charge, to drop
On headlong Appetite, the slackned rein,
And give us up to License, unrecall'd,   260

146

Unmarkt; – See, from behind her secret stand,
The sly Informer minutes every Fault,
And her dread Diary with Horror fills:
Not the gross Act alone employs her Pen;
She reconnoitres Fancy's airy band,
A watchful Foe! The formidable Spy,
List'ning o'erhears the Whispers of our Camp;
Our dawning Purposes of Heart explores,
And steals our Embryos of Iniquity.
As all-rapacious Usurers conceal   270
Their Doomsday book from all-consuming Heirs;
Thus, with Indulgence most severe, She treats
Us, Spendthrifts of inestimable Time;
Unnoted, notes each Moment misapply'd;
In leaves more durable than leaves of Brass,
Writes our whole History; which Death shall read
In every pale Delinquent's private Ear;
And Judgement publish; Publish to more worlds
Than this; and endless Age in groans resound.
Lorenzo, such that Sleeper in thy Breast!   280
Such is her Slumber; and her Vengeance such
For slighted Counsel; such thy future Peace!
And thin'st thou still canst be wise too soon?
    But why on Time So lavish is my Song?
On this great Theme kind Nature keeps a School,
To teach her Sons Herself. Each Night we Dye,
Each Morn are born anew; Each Day, a Life!
And shall we kill each Day? If Trifling kills;
Sure Vice must butcher. O what heaps of slain
Cry out for Vengeance on us! Time destroy'd   290
Is Suicide, where more than Blood is spilt
Time flies, Death urges, Knells call, Heaven invites,
Hell threatens; All exerts; in Effort, All;
More than Creation labours! – Labours more?
And is there in Creation, What, amidst
This Tumult Universal, wing'd Dispatch;
And ardent Energy, supinely yawns? –

Man sleeps; and Man alone; and Man, whose Fate,
Fate irreversible, entire, extreme,
Endless, hair-hung, breeze-shaken, o'er the Gulph   300
A moment trembles; drops: and Man, for whom
All else is in alarm: Man, the sole Cause
Of this surrounding Storm! and yet he sleeps,
As the Storm rock'd to rest. – Throw Years away?
Throw Empires, and be blameless. Moments seize,
Heaven's on their Wing: a Moment we may wish,
When Worlds want Wealth to buy. Bid Day stand still,
Bid him drive back his Carr, and reimport
The Period past; regive the given hour.
Lorenzo, more than Miracles we want: 310
Lorenzo – O for Yesterdays to come!

*

Who venerate themselves, the World despise.
For what, gay friend! is this escutcheon'd World,
Which hangs out Death in one eternal Night?
A Night, that glooms us in the Noon-tide Ray,
And wraps our Thought, at Banquets, in the Shroud.
Life's little stage is a small Eminence,   360
Inch-high the Grave above; that Home of Man,
Where dwells the Multitude, we gaze around;
We read their Monuments; we sigh; and while
We sigh, we sink; and are what we deplor'd;
Lamenting, or Lamented all our Lot!

*

Art thou so moor'd thou canst not disengage,
Nor give thy Thoughts a ply to future scenes?   390
Since, by Life's passing breath, blown up from Earth,
Light, as the Summer's dust, we take in Air
A Moment's giddy flight; and fall again;
Join the dull Mass, increase the trodden Soil,

148

⌊And sleep till Earth herself shall be no more;
Since Then (as Emmets their small World o'erthrown)
We, sore-amaz'd, from out Earth's Ruins crawl,
And rise to Fate extreme, of Foul or Fair,
As Man's own Choice, Controuler of the Skies!

*

Hast thou no Friend to set thy mind abroach?
Good Sense will Stagnate:⌈Thoughts shut up want Air,
✕And spoil, like Bales unopen'd to the Sun.
Had Thought been All, sweet Speech had been deny'd;
Speech, Thought's Canal! Speech, Thought's Criterion too!
Thought, in the Mine, may come forth Gold or Dross;   470
When coin'd in Word, we know its real worth.
If Sterling; store it for thy future Use;
'Twill buy thee Benefit; perhaps, Renown.
Thought, too, deliver'd, is the more possest;
Teaching, we learn; and giving, we retain
The Births of Intellect: when dumb, forgot.
Speech ventilates our Intellectual fire;
Speech burnishes our Mental Magazine:
Brightens for Ornament; and whets for Use:
What Numbers, sheath'd in Erudition lie,   480
Plung'd to the Hilts in venerable Tomes,
And rusted in; who might have born an Edge,
And play'd a sprightly beam, if born to Speech;
If born blest Heirs of half their Mother's tongue?
'Tis Thought's exchange, which like th'alternate Push
Of waves conflicting, breaks the learned Scum,
And defecates the Student's standing Pool.

*

⌈ Whatever Farce the boastful Hero plays,
⌊Virtue alone has Majesty in Death;   650
And greater still, the more the Tyrant frowns.

149

Philander! He severely frown'd on Thee.
'No warning given! Unceremonious Fate!
A suddain Rush from Life's meridian Joys!
A Wrench from all we Love! from all we are!
A restless bed of Pain! a Plunge opaque
Beyond Conjecture! Feeble Nature's dread!
Strong Reason's shudder at the dark Unknown!
A Sun extinguisht, a just opening Grave!
And oh! the last, last; what? can words express?   660
Thought reach it? the last – Silence of a Friend!'

NIGHT THE THIRD

   Song, beauty, youth, love, virtue, joy! this Group
Of bright Ideas, Flowers of Paradise,
As yet unforfeit! in one blaze we bind,
Kneel, and present it to the Skies; as All
We guess of Heaven: And these were all her Own:
And she was mine; and I was – was – most blest, –
Gay Title of the deepest Misery!   100
As bodies grow more pond'rous, rob'd of Life;
Good lost weighs more in Grief, than Gain'd, in Joy.
Like blossom'd Trees o'erturn'd by vernal Storm,
Lovely in Death the beauteous Ruin lay;
And if in Death still lovely, lovelier There;
Far lovlier! Pity swells the Tide of Love.
And will not the Severe excuse a Sigh?
Scorn the proud Man that is asham'd to weep;
Our Tears indulg'd indeed deserve our Shame.
Ye that e're lost an Angel! pity me.   110

                          *

For, oh the curst Ungodliness of Zeal!
While sinful Flesh relented, Spirit nurst
In blind Infallibility's embrace,
The Sainted Spirit petrify'd the breast:

                         150

Deny'd the Charity of Dust, to spread
O'er Dust! a charity their Dogs enjoy.   170
What cou'd I do? what Succour? what Resource?
With pious Sacrilege, a Grave I stole;
With impious Piety, that Grave I wrong'd;
Short in my Duty! Coward in my Grief!
More like her Murderer, than Friend, I crept
With soft-suspended Step, and muffled deep
In midnight Darkness, whisper'd my Last Sigh.
I whisper'd what should echo thro' their realms;
Nor writ her Name, whose tomb shou'd pierce the Skies.
Presumptuous Fear! How durst I dread her Foes,   180
While Nature's loudest Dictates I obey'd?
Pardon Necessity, Blest Shade! Of Grief,
And Indignation rival bursts I pour'd;
Half-execration mingled with my Pray'r;
Kindled at man, while I his God ador'd;
Sore-grudg'd the Savage land her Sacred Dust;
Stampt the curst Soil; and with Humanity
(Denied Narcissa,) wisht them All a Grave.

*

Our dying Friends come o'er us like a Cloud,
To damp our brainless Ardors; and abate
That Glare of Life, which often blinds the Wise.
Our dying Friends are Pioneers, to smooth   280
Our rugged Pass to Death; to break those Bars
Of Terror, and Abhorrence, Nature throws
Cross our obstructed way; and, thus, to make
Wellcome, as Safe, our Port from every Storm.
Each Friend by Fate snatcht from us, is a Plume
Pluckt from the wing of human Vanity,
Which makes us stoop from our aeriel Heights,
And dampt with Omen of our own Decease,
On drooping pinions of Ambition lower'd,
Just skim Earth's Surface, ere we break it up,   290

151

O'er putrid Earth to scratch a little Dust,
And save the World a Nuisance.

*

Ere man has measured half his weary Stage,
His Luxuries have left him no reserve,
No maiden Relishes, unbroacht Delights;
On cold-serv'd Repetitions He subsists,
And in the tasteless Present chews the Past;   320
Disgusted chews, and scarce can swallow down.
Like lavish Ancestors, his earlier Years
Have disinherited his future Hours,
Which starve on Oughts, and glean their former Field.
 Live ever Here, Lorenzo! – shocking Thought!
So shocking, they who wish, disown it, too;
Disown from shame, what they from Folly crave.
Live ever in the Womb, nor see the Light?
For what live ever Here? With labouring Step
To tread our former Footsteps? Pace the Round   330
Eternal? To climb Life's worn, heavy wheel,
Which draws up nothing new? To beat, and beat,
The beaten Track? To bid each wretched day
The Former mock; To surfeit on the Same,
And yawn our Joys? or thank a Misery
For Change, tho' sad? To see what we have seen?
Hear, till unheard the same old Slobber'd Tale?
To taste the tasted, and at each return
Less tastful? O'er our Palates to decant
Another Vintage? strain a flatter year,   340
Thro' loaded Vessels, and a laxer Tone?
Crazy Machines to grind Earth's wasted Fruits!
Ill-ground, and worse concocted; Load, not Life!
The Rational foul Kennels of Excess!
Still-streaming Thorough fairs of dull Debauch!
Trembling each Gulp, lest Death should snatch the Bowl.

*

152

Life makes the Soul Dependent on the Dust;
Death gives her wings to mount above the Spheres:
Thro' Chinks, styl'd Organs, dim Life peeps at light;   450
Death bursts th' Involving Cloud, and all is Day:
All Eye, all Ear, the disembody'd Power.
Death has feign'd Evils, Nature shall not feel;
Life, Ills substantial, Wisdom cannot shun.
Is not the mighty Mind, that Son of Heaven!
By tyrant Life, dethron'd, imprison'd, pain'd?
By Death enlarg'd, ennobled, Deify'd?
Death but entombs the Body; Life the Soul.

NIGHT THE FOURTH
Why start at Death? Where is he? Death arriv'd,
Is past; not come, or gone, He's never here.
E'er Hope, Sensation fails; Black-boding Man
Receives, not suffers, Death's tremendous Blow.
The Knell, the Shroud, the Mattock and the Grave;   10
The deep damp Vault, the Darkness, and the Worm;
These are the Bugbears of a Winter's Eve,
The Terrors of the Living, not the Dead.
Imagination's Fool, and Error's Wretch,
Man makes a Death, which Nature never made;
Then on the Point of his own Fancy falls;
And feels a thousand Deaths, in fearing one.

*

A Time there is, when, like a thrice-told Tale,
Long-rifled Life of Sweet can yield no more,
But from our Comment on the Comedy,
Pleasing Reflections on Parts well-sustain'd,   40
Or purpos'd Emendations where we fail'd,
Or Hopes of Plaudits from our candid Judge,
When, on their Exit, Souls are bid unrobe,

153

✕Toss Fortune back her Tinsel, and her Plume,
And drop this Mask of Flesh behind the Scene.

*

The World's a stately Bark, on dangerous Seas,
With Pleasure seen, but boarded at our Peril;
Here, on a single Plank, thrown safe ashore,
I hear the Tumult of the distant Throng,
As that of Seas remote, or dying Storms;
And meditate on Scenes, more silent still;
Pursue my Theme, and fight the Fear of Death.
Here, like a Shepherd gazing from his Hut,
Touching his Reed, or leaning on his Staff,   90
Eager Ambition's fiery Chace I see;
I see the circling Hunt, of noisy Men,
Burst Laws Enclosure, leap the Mounds of Right,
Pursuing and pursued, each other's Prey;
As Wolves, for Rapine; as the Fox, for Wiles;
Till Death, that mighty Hunter, earths them all.

*

O Thou great Arbiter of Life and Death!
Nature's immortal, immaterial Sun!
Whose all-prolific Beam late call'd me forth   140
From Darkness, teeming Darkness, where I lay
The Worms inferior, and, in Rank, beneath
The Dust I tread on, high to bear my Brow,
To drink the Spirit of the golden Day,
And triumph in Existence; and could'st know
No Motive, but my Bliss; and hast ordain'd
A Rise in Blessing! with the Patriarch's Joy,
Thy Call I follow to the Land unknown;
I trust in thee, and know in whom I trust;
Or Life, or Death, is equal; neither weighs,   150
All Weight in this – O let me live to Thee!

*

154

And is Devotion Virtue? 'Tis compell'd;
What Heart of Stone, but glows at Thoughts, like These?   260
Such Contemplations mount us; and shou'd mount
The Mind still higher; nor ever glance on Man,
Unraptur'd, uninflam'd. – Where rowl my Thoughts
To rest from Wonders? Other Wonders rise,
And strike where'er they rowl; My Soul is caught;
Heav'n's sovereign Blessings, clust'ring from the Cross,
Rush on her, in a Throng, and close her round,
The Prisoner of Amaze!

NIGHT THE FIFTH
By Day, the Soul o'erborn by Life's Career,
Stunn'd by the Din, and giddy with the Glare,
Reels far from Reason, jostled by the Throng.
By Day the Soul is passive, all her Thoughts
Impos'd, precarious, broken, e'er mature.
By Night, from Objects free, from Passion cool,   120
Thoughts uncontroul'd, and unimpress'd, the Births
Of pure Election, arbitrary range,
Not to the Limits of one World confin'd;
But from Etherial Travels light on Earth,
As Voyagers drop Anchor, for Repose.
   Let Indians, and the Gay, like Indians, fond
Of feather'd Fopperies, the Sun adore:
Darkness has more Divinity for me;
It strikes Thought inward, it drives back the Soul
To settle on Herself, our Point supreme!   130

*

Hail, precious Moments! stol'n from the black Waste
Of murder'd Time! Auspicious Midnight! Hail!
The World excluded, every Passion hush'd,
And open'd a calm Intercourse with Heav'n,
Here, the Soul sits in Council, ponders past,

155

Predestines future Actions; sees, not feels,
Tumultuous Life; and reasons with the Storm;   200
All her Lies answers, and thinks down her Charms.
    What awful Joy? what mental Liberty?
I am not pent in Darkness; rather say
(If not too bold) in Darkness I'm embower'd.
Delightful Gloom! the clust'ring Thoughts around
Spontaneous rise, and blossom in the Shade;
But droop by Day, and sicken in the Sun.

*

Is it, that Time steals on with downy Feet,
Nor wakes Indulgence from her Golden Dream?
To-day is so like yesterday, it cheats;   400
We take the lying Sister for the same.
Life glides away, Lorenzo! like a Brook;
For ever changing, unperceiv'd the Change.
In the same Brook none ever bath'd him twice:
To the same Life none ever twice awoke.
We call the Brook the same; the same we think
Our Life, tho' still more rapid in its Flow;
Nor mark the Much irrevocably laps'd,
And mingled with the Sea. Or shall we say
(Retaining still the Brook to bear us on)   410
That Life is like a Vessel on the Stream?
In Life embark'd, we smoothly down the Tide
Of Time descend, but not on Time intent;
Amus'd, unconscious of the gliding Wave;
Till on a sudden we perceive a Shock;
We start, awake, look out; what see we there?
Our brittle Bark is burst on Charon's shore.

*

    Must I then forward only look for Death?
Backward I turn mine Eye, and find him there.   710
Man is a Self-survivor ev'ry Year.

156

Man, like a Stream, is in perpetual Flow.
Death's a destroyer of Quotidian prey.
My Youth, my Noon-tide, His; my Yesterday;
The bold Invader shares the present Hour.
Each Moment on the former shuts the Grave.
While Man is growing, Life is in Decrease;
And Cradles rock us nearer to the Tomb.
Our Birth is nothing but our Death begun;
As Tapers wast, that Instant they take Fire.   720

                              *

Thus runs Death's dread Commission: 'Strike, but so,
As most alarms the Living by the Dead'.   810
Hence Stratagem delights him, and Surprize,
And cruel sport with Man's Securities...
    The dreadful Masquerader, thus equipt,   860
Out-Sallies on Adventures. Ask you where?
Where is He not? For his peculiar haunts,
Let this suffice; sure as Night follows Day,
Death treads in Pleasure's footsteps round the World,
When Pleasure treads the Paths, which Reason shuns.
When, against Reason, Riot shuts the door,
And Gayety supplies the Place of Sense,
Then foremost at the Banquet, and the Ball,
Death leads the Dance, or stamps the deadly Die;
Nor ever fails the Midnight Bowl to crown.   870
Gayly carousing to his gay Compeers,
Inly he laughs, to see them laugh at him,
As Absent far; and when the Revel burns,
When Fear is banisht, and triumphant Thought,
Calling for all the Joys beneath the Moon,
Against Him turns the Key; and bids him Sup
With their progenitors, – He drops his Mask,
Frowns out at full; they start, despair, expire.
    Scarce with more sudden Terror and Surprize,
From His black Masque of Nitre, touch'd by Fire,   880

157

He bursts, expands, roars, blazes, and devours.
And is not this triumphant Treachery,
And more than simple Conquest in the Fiend?

*

See, high in Air, the sportive Goddess hangs,
Unlocks her Casket, spreads her glitt'ring Ware,
And calls the giddy Winds to puff abroad   960
Her random Bounties, o'er the gaping Throng.
All rush rapacious; Friends o'er trodden Friends;
Sons o'er their Fathers, Subjects o'er their Kings,
Priests o'er their Gods, and Lovers o'er the Fair,
Still more adored, to snatch the golden Show'r.
✗ Gold glitters most, where Virtue shines no more;
As Stars from absent Suns have leave to shine.
O what a pretious Pack of Votaries,
Unkennell'd from the Prisons, and the Stews,
Pour in, all opening in their Idol's Praise!   970
All, ardent, eye, each Wafture of her Hand,
And, wide-expanding their voracious Jaws,
Morsel on Morsel swallow down unchew'd,
Untasted, thro' mad Appetite for more;
Gorg'd to the throat, yet lean and ravenous still.
Sagacious All, to trace the smallest Game,
And bold to seize the Greatest. If (blest Chance!)
Court-Zephyrs sweetly breath, they launch, they fly
O'er Just, o'er Sacred, all forbidden Ground,
Drunk with the burning Scent of Place, or Pow'r,   980
Staunch to the foot of Lucre, till they die.

NIGHT THE SIXTH
   Nor dreadful our Transition; tho' the Mind,
An Artist at creating self-alarms,   50
Rich in Expedients for Inquietude,
Is prone to paint it dreadful. Who can take

158

Death's Portrait true? the Tyrant never sate.
Our Sketch, all random Strokes, Conjecture all;
Close shuts the Grave, nor tells one single Tale.
Death, and his Image rising in the Brain,
Bear faint resemblance; never are alike;
Fear shakes the Pencil, Fancy loves Excess,
Dark Ignorance is lavish of her Shades;
And These the formidable Picture draw.   60

*

How Great (while yet we tread the kindred Clod,
And ev'ry Moment fear to sink beneath
The Clod we tread; soon trodden by our Sons,)
How Great in the wild Whirl of Time's pursuits
To stop, and pause, involv'd in high Presage,
Thro' the long Visto of a thousand Years,
To stand contemplating our distant Selves,
As in a magnifying Mirror seen,
Enlarg'd, Ennobl'd, Elevate, Divine?   120
To prophesy our own Futurities?
To gaze in Thought on what all Thought transcends?
To talk, with Fellow-Candidates, of Joys
As far beyond Conception, as Desert,
Ourselves the astonish'd Talkers, and the Tale!

*

    If inextinguishable Thirst in Man
To know; how rich, how full our Banquet There?
There, not the Moral world alone unfolds;
The World Material lately seen in Shades,
And in those Shades, by Fragments, only seen,
And seen those Fragments by the labouring Eye,
Unbroken, then, illustrious and entire,   170
Its ample Sphere, its universal Frame,
Its full Dimensions, swells to the Survey;

And enters, at one Glance, the ravisht Sight.
From some superior Point (where, who can tell?
Suffice it, 'tis a Point where Gods reside)
How shall the stranger Man's illumin'd Eye,
In the vast Ocean of unbounded Space,
Behold an Infinite of floating Worlds
Divide the Crystal Waves of Ether pure,
In endless Voyage, without Port? The least   180
Of these disseminated Orbs, how Great?
Great as they are, what Numbers These surpass
Huge, as Leviathan, to that small Race,
Those twinkling Multitudes of little Life,
He swallows unperceiv'd? Stupendous These!
Yet what are these Stupendous to the Whole?
As Particles, as Atoms ill-perceiv'd;
As circulating Globules in our Veins;
So vast the Plan: Fecundity Divine!
Exuberant Source! perhaps, I wrong thee still.   190

*

Ambition! powerful source of Good and Ill!
Thy strength in Man, like length of wing in Birds,   400
When disengag'd from Earth, with greater Ease
And swifter Flight, transports us to the skies:
By Toys entangled, or in Guilt bemir'd,
It turns a Curse; it is our Chain, and Scourge,
In this dark Dungeon, where confin'd we lie,
Close-grated by the sordid Bars of Sense;
All prospect of Eternity shut out;
And, but for Execution, ne'er set Free,
    With error in Ambition justly charg'd,
Find we Lorenzo wiser in his Wealth?   410
What if thy Rental I reform? and draw
An Inventory new to set thee right?
Where, thy true Treasure? Gold says, 'not in me,'
And, 'not in me,' the Diamond. Gold is poor;

India's insolvent: Seek it in Thyself;
Seek in thy naked Self, and find it There.
In Being so Descended, Form'd, Endow'd;
Sky-born, sky-guided, sky-returning Race!
Erect, Immortal, Rational, Divine!
In Senses, which inherit Earth, and Heavens;   420
Enjoy the various riches Nature yields;
Far nobler! give the riches they enjoy;
Give tast to Fruits; and harmony to Groves;
Their radiant beams to Gold, and Gold's bright Sire;
Take in, at once, the Landscape of the world,
At a small Inlet, which a Grain might close,
And half create the wondrous World, they see.
Our Senses, as our Reason, are Divine.
But for the magic Organ's powerful charm,
Earth were a rude, uncolour'd Chaos still.   430
Objects are but the Occasion; Ours th' Exploit;
Ours is the Cloth, the Pencil, and the Paint,
Which Nature's admirable Picture draws;
And beautifies Creation's ample Dome.
Like Milton's Eve, when gazing on the Lake,
Man makes the matchless Image, man admires.
Say then, shall man, his Thoughts all sent abroad,
Superior wonders in Himself forgot,
His Admiration wast on objects round,
When Heaven makes Him the soul of all he sees?   440
Absurd! not Rare! so Great, so Mean, is man.

*

Doubt you this Truth? Why labours your Belief?
If Earth's whole Orb, by some due-distanc'd eye,
Were seen at once, her tow'ring Alps would sink,
And level'd Atlas leave an even Sphere.
Thus Earth, and all that earthly minds admire,
Is swallow'd in Eternity's vast Round.
To that stupendous view, when souls awake,   600

161

So large of late, so mountainous to man,
Time's Toys subside; and equal All below.

*

Look Nature through, 'tis Revolution All.
All Change, no Death. Day follows Night; and Night
The dying Day; Stars, rise, and set, and rise;
Earth take th' Example. See, the Summer gay,   680
With her green chaplet, and ambrosial flow'rs,
Droops into pallid Autumn: Winter grey,
Horrid with frost, and turbulent with storm,
Blows Autumn, and his golden fruits away,
Then melts into the Spring: Soft Spring, with breath
Favonian, from warm chambers of the South,
Recalls the First. All, to reflourish, fades.
As in a wheel, All sinks, to reascend.
Emblems of man, who passes, not expires.
    With this minute distinction, Emblems just,   690
Nature revolves, but Man advances; Both
Eternal, that a Circle, this a Line.
That gravitates, this soars. Th' aspiring soul
Ardent, and tremulous, like Flame, ascends;
Zeal, and Humility, her wings to Heaven.
The world of Matter, with its various Forms,
All dies into new Life. Life born from Death
Rolls the vast Mass, and shall for ever roll.

NIGHT THE SEVENTH
    Shall sons of Æther, shall the Blood of Heav'n,
Set up their Hopes on Earth, and stable here,
With brutal Acquiescence in the Mire?
Lorenzo, no! they shall be nobly pain'd;
The glorious Foreigners, distrest, shall sigh
On Thrones; and Thou congratulate the Sigh:
Man's Misery declares him born for Bliss;   60

162

His anxious Heart asserts the Truth I sing,
And gives the Sceptic in his Head the Lye.

*

Man's Heart eats all Things, and is hungry still;
'More, more,' the Glutton cries: For something New
So rages Appetite, if man can't Mount,
He will Descend. He starves on the Possest.
Hence, the World's Master, from Ambition's Spire,
In Caprea plung'd; and div'd beneath the Brute
In that rank Sty why wallow'd Empire's Son
Supreme? because he could no higher fly;
His Riot was Ambition in Despair.   130

*

Could I believe Lorenzo's system true,   651
In this black Channel would my Ravings run: . . .
'O for Delusion! O for Error still!   663
Could Vengeance strike much stronger, than to plant
A Thinking Being in a World like This,
Not over-rich before, now beggar'd quite;
More curst than at the Fall? The Sun goes out!
The Thorns shoot up! What Thorns in ev'ry Thought!
Why Sense of Better? It imbitters Worse.
Why Sense? why Life? If but to sigh, then sink   670
To what I was? Twice Nothing! and much Woe!
Woe, from Heav'n's Bounties! Woe, from what was wont
To flatter most, high Intellectual Pow'rs.
Thought, Virtue, Knowledge! Blessings, by thy Scheme,
All poison'd into Pains. First, Knowledge, once
My Soul's Ambition, now her greatest Dread.
To know myself, true Wisdom? – No, to shun
That shocking Science, Parent of Despair!
Avert thy Mirror; If I see, I die!

*

163

Duty! Religion! – These, our Duty done,
Imply Reward. Religion is Mistake.
Duty? – There's none, but to repel the Cheat.
Ye Cheats! away; ye Daughters of my Pride!
Who feign yourselves the Fav'rites of the Skies: 720
Ye tow'ring Hopes! abortive Energies!
That toss, and struggle, in my lying Breast,
To scale the Skies, and build Presumptions There,
As I were Heir of an Eternity;
Vain, vain Ambitions! trouble me no more.
Why travel far in Quest of sure Defeat?
As bounded as my Being, be my Wish.
All is inverted, Wisdom is a Fool.
Sense! take the Rein! blind Passion! drive us on;
And, Ignorance! befriend us on our Way;   730
Ye new, but truest Patrons of our Peace!
Yes; give the Pulse full Empire; live the Brute,
Since, as the Brute, we die. The Sum of Man,
Of Godlike man! to revel, and to rot.

*

O give Eternity! or Thought destroy. –
But without Thought our Curse were half unfelt;
Its blunted edge would spare the throbbing Heart . . .   764

*

How the Grave's alter'd? Fathomless, as Hell!
A real Hell to Those who dreamt of Heav'n.
Annihilation! How it yawns before me?
Next Moment I may drop from Thought, from Sense,   820
The Privilege of Angels, and of Worms,
An Outcast from Existence! And this Spirit,
This all-pervading, this all-conscious Soul,
This Particle of Energy divine,
Which travels Nature, flies from Star to Star,

164

And visits Gods, and emulates their Pow'rs,
For ever is extinguisht. Horror! Death!
Death of that Death I fearless, once, survey'd.
When Horror Universal shall descend,
And Heaven's dark Concave urn all Human Race,   830
On that enormous, unrefunding Tomb,
How just this Verse? this monumental Sigh!
  Beneath the Lumber of demolisht Worlds,
  Deep in the Rubbish of the gen'ral Wreck,
  Swept Ignominious to the common Mass
  Of Matter, never dignify'd with Life,
  Here lie proud Rationals; The Sons of Heav'n!
  The Lords of Earth! The Property of Worms!
  Beings of Yesterday, and no To-morrow!
  Who lived in Terror, and in Pangs expir'd!   840
  All gone to rot in Chaos; or, to make
  Their happy Transit into Blocks, or Brutes,
  No longer sully their Creator's name.

NIGHT THE EIGHTH
A World, where Lust of Pleasure, Grandeur, Gold,
Three Daemons that divide its Realms between them,   55
With Strokes alternate buffet to and fro,
Man's restless Heart, their Sport, their flying Ball;
Till, with its giddy Circle, sick, and tir'd,
It pants for Peace, and drops into Despair:

        *

What wondrous Prize has kindled this Career,
Stuns, with the Din, and choaks us, with the Dust,
On Life's gay Stage, one Inch above the Grave?
The Proud run up and down in quest of Eyes;
The Sensual in pursuit of something worse;   90
The Grave, of Gold; the Politic, of Power;
And All, of other Butterflies, as vain!

165

As Eddies draw things frivolous, and light,
How is Man's Heart by Vanity drawn in;
On the swift Circle of returning Toys,
Whirl'd, Straw-like, round and round, and then ingulph'd;
Where gay Delusion darkens to Despair!

*

Self-flatter'd, unexperienc'd, high in Hope,   180
When Young, with sanguine Cheer, and Streamers gay,
We cut our Cable, launch into the World,
And fondly dream each Wind, and Star, our Friend;
All, in some darling Enterprize embarkt:
But where is he can fathom its Extent?
Amid a Multitude of artless Hands,
Ruin's sure Perquisite! her lawful Prize!
Some steer aright; but the black Blast blows hard,
And puffs them wide of Hope: With Hearts of Proof,
Full against Wind, and Tide, some win their Way;   190
And when strong Effort has deserv'd the Port,
And tugg'd it into View, 'tis won! 'tis lost!
Tho' strong their Oar, still stronger is their Fate,
They Strike; and while they Triumph, they Expire.
In Stress of Weather, Most; Some sink outright;
O'er them, and o'er their Names the Billows close;
To-morrow knows not they were ever Born:

*

Florello lately cast on this rude Coast,
A helpless Infant; now, a heedless Child;
To poor Clarissa's Throes, thy Care succeeds;
Care full of Love, and yet severe as Hate:
O'er thy Soul's Joy how oft thy Fondness frowns?
Needful Austerities his Will restrain;   250
As Thorns fence in the tender Plant from Harm.
As yet, his Reason cannot go alone,

166

But asks a sterner Nurse to lead it on:
His little Heart is often terrify'd;
The Blush of Morning in his Cheek, turns pale;
Its pearly Dew-drop trembles in his Eye;
His harmless Eye! and drowns an Angel there:
Ah! what avails his Innocence? The Task
Injoin'd, must discipline his early Pow'rs;
He learns to sigh, ere he is known to sin;   260
Guiltless, and sad! A Wretch before the Fall!
How cruel this! More cruel to forbear.
Our Nature such, with necessary Pains,
We purchase Prospects of precarious Peace:
Tho' not a Father, This might steal a Sigh.

*

See, the steel'd Files of season'd Veterans,
Train'd to the World, in burnisht Falshood bright;
Deep in the fatal Strategems of Peace;
All soft Sensation, in the Throng, rubb'd off;
All their keen Purpose, in Politeness, sheath'd;
His Friends eternal – during Interest;
His Foes implacable, – when worth their While;
At War with ev'ry Welfare, but their own;
As wise as Lucifer; and half as Good;
And by whom, none, but Lucifer, can gain –   300
Naked, through These (so common Fate ordains),
Naked of Heart, his cruel Course he runs,
Stung out of All, most amiable in Life,
Prompt Truth, and open Thought, and Smiles unfeign'd;
Affection, as his Species, wide-diffus'd;
Noble Presumptions to Mankind's Renown;
Ingenuous Trust, and Confidence of Love.
    These Claims to Joy (if Mortals Joy might claim)
Will cost him many a Sigh; till Time, and Pains,
From the slow Mistress of this School, Experience,   310
And her Assistant, pausing, pale Distrust,

167

Purchase a dear-bought Clue to lead his Youth,
Thro' serpentine Obliquities of life,
And the dark Labyrinth of human Hearts...
The World's all Title-Page, there's no Contents;
The World's all Face; the Man who shews his Heart,
Is hooted for his Nudities, and scorn'd. 335

*

An Eminence, though fancy'd, turns the Brain;
All Vice wants Hellebore; but, of all Vice,
Pride loudest calls, and for the largest Bowl;
Because, all other Vice unlike, it flies,
In Fact, the Point, in Fancy, most pursu'd.
Who court Applause, oblige the World in this;
They gratify Man's Passion to refuse:
Superior Honour when assum'd, is lost; 520
E'en Good Men turn Banditti, and rejoice,
Like Kouli-Kan, in Plunder of the Proud.

*

Think you there's but One Whoredom? Whoredom, All,
But when our Reason licenses Delight: 550
Dost doubt, Lorenzo? Thou shalt doubt no more:
Thy Father chides thy Gallantries, yet hugs
An ugly, common Harlot, in the Dark;
A rank Adulterer with others Gold;
And that Hag, Vengeance, in a Corner, charms;
Hatred her Brothel has, as well as Love,
Where horrid Epicures debauch in Blood;
Whate'er the Motive, Pleasure is the Mark:
For Her, the black Assassin draws his Sword;
For Her, dark Statesmen trim their Midnight Lamp, 560
To which no single Sacrifice may fall;
For Her, the Saint abstains; the Miser starves;
The Stoic proud, for Pleasure, Pleasure scorn'd;

For Her, Affliction's Daughters Grief indulge,
And find, or hope, a Luxury in Tears;
For Her, Guilt, Shame, Toil, Danger, we defy;
And, with an Aim voluptuous, rush on Death.
Thus universal her despotic Pow'r.

*

No Man e'er found a happy Life by Chance,
Or yawn'd it into Being, with a Wish;
Or, with the Snout of grov'ling Appetite,   615
E'er smelt it out, and grubb'd it from the Dirt;
An Art it is, and must be learnt; and learnt
With unremitting Effort, or be lost;

*

Some Angel guide my Pencil, while I draw,
What nothing less than Angel can exceed.   1080
A Man on Earth devoted to the Skies,
Like Ships in Seas, while in, above the World.
With Aspect mild, and elevated Eye,
Behold him seated on a Mount serene,
Above the Fogs of Sense, and Passion's Storm;
All the black Cares, and Tumults, of This Life,
Like harmless Thunders, breaking at his Feet,
Excite his Pity, not impair his Peace:
Earth's genuine Sons, the Sceptred, and the Slave,
A mingled Mob! A wand'ring Herd! he sees   1090
Bewilder'd in the Vale; in All unlike!
His full Reverse in All! What higher Praise?
What stronger Demonstration of the Right?
The Present all Their Care, the Future, His.
When Public Welfare calls, or Private Want,
They give to Fame; His Bounty He conceals:
Their Virtues varnish Nature; His, exalt:
Mankind's Esteem They court; and He, his Own:

Theirs, the wild Chace of false Felicities;
His, the compos'd Possession of the true: 1100
Alike thro'out is His consistent Peace,
All of one Colour, and an even Thread;
While party-colour'd Shreds of Happiness,
With hideous Gaps between, patch up for Them
A Madman's Robe; each Puff of Fortune blows
The Tatters by, and shews their Nakedness.
    He sees with other Eyes than Theirs: Where They
Behold a Sun, He spies a Deity;
What makes Them only Smile, makes Him Adore;
Where They see Mountains, He but Atoms sees;   1110
An Empire, in His Balance, weighs a Grain:
They Things Terrestrial worship, as Divine;
His Hopes Immortal blow them by, as Dust,
That dims his Sight, and shortens his Survey,
Which longs, in Infinite, to lose all Bound:

NIGHT THE NINTH
As when a Traveller, a long Day past
In painful Search of what he cannot find,
At Night's Approach, content with the next Cot,
There ruminates, awhile, his Labour lost;
Then, chears his Heart with what his Fate affords,
And chaunts his Sonnet to deceive the Time,
Till the due Season calls him to Repose:
Thus I, long-travell'd in the Ways of Men,
And dancing, with the rest, the giddy Maze,
Where Disappointment smiles at Hope's Career,   10
Warn'd by the Langour of Life's Ev'ning Ray,
At length, have hous'd me in a humble Shed;
Where, future Wand'ring banish'd from my Thought,
And waiting, patient, the sweet Hour of Rest;
I chase the Moments with a serious Song:
Song sooths our Pains; and Age has Pains to sooth.

*

170

Seest thou, Lorenzo! what depends on Man?
The Fate of Nature; as for Man, her Birth.
Earth's Actors change Earth's transitory Scenes,
And make Creation groan with human Guilt:
How must it groan, in a new Deluge whelm'd;
But not of Waters? At the destin'd Hour,
By the loud Trumpet summon'd to the Charge,
See, all the formidable Sons of Fire,
Eruptions, Earthquakes, Comets, Lightnings, play   160
Their various Engines; All at once disgorge
Their blazing Magazines; and take, by Storm,
This poor terrestrial Citadel of Man.
    Amazing Period! when each Mountain-Height
Out-burns Vesuvius; Rocks eternal pour
Their melted Mass, as Rivers once they pour'd;
Stars rush; and final Ruin fiercely drives
Her Ploughshare o'er Creation! – While aloft,
More than Astonishment! if more can be!
Far other Firmament than e'er was seen,   170
Than e'er was thought by Man! Far other Stars!
Stars animate, that govern these of Fire;
Far other Sun! – A Sun, O how unlike
The Babe at Bethle'm! How unlike the Man
Thon groan'd on Calvary! – Yet He it is;
That Man of Sorrows! O how chang'd? What Pomp?
In Grandeur Terrible, All Heav'n descends!
And Gods, ambitious, triumph in His Train,
A swift Archangel, with his golden Wing,
As Blots and Clouds, that darken and disgrace   180
The Scene divine, sweeps Stars and Suns aside:
And now, all Dross remov'd, Heav'n's own pure Day,
Full on the Confines of our Æther, flames:
While (dreadful Contrast!) far, how far beneath!
Hell, bursting, belches forth her blazing Seas,
And Storms sulphureous; her voracious Jaws
Expanding wide, and roaring for her Prey.

*

Shall Man alone, whose Fate, whose final Fate,
Hangs on That Hour, exclude it from his Thought?
I think of nothing else; I see! I feel it!
All Nature, like an Earthquake, trembling round!
All Deities, like Summer's Swarms, on Wing!
All basking in the full Meridian Blaze!
I see the Judge inthron'd! The flaming Guard!
The Volume open'd! Open'd every Heart!
A Sun-Beam pointing out each secret Thought!   270
No Patron! Intercessor none! Now past
The sweet, the clement, Mediatorial Hour!
For Guilt no Plea! To Pain, no Pause! no Bound!
Inexorable, All! and All, Extreme!

*

Time, this vast Fabric for him built, (and doom'd
With him to fall) now bursting o'er his Head;
His Lamp, the Sun, extinguish'd; from beneath   300
The Frown of hideous Darkness, calls his Sons
From their long Slumber; from Earth's heaving Womb
To second Birth; contemporary Throng!
Rouz'd at One Call; upstarted from One Bed;
Prest in one Croud; appall'd with One Amaze;
He turns them o'er, Eternity! to thee:
Then (as a King depos'd disdains to live),
He falls on his own Scythe; nor falls alone;
His greatest Foe falls with him; Time, and He
Who murder'd all Time's Offspring, Death, expire.   310

*

To see the mighty Dramatist's last Act
(As meet) in Glory rising o'er the rest:
No fancy'd God, a God indeed, descends,   360
To solve all Knots; to strike the Moral home;
To throw full Day on darkest scenes of Time;

To clear, commend, exalt, and crown the Whole:
Hence, in one Peal of loud, eternal Praise,
The charm'd Spectators thunder their Applause,
And the vast Void beyond, Applause resounds.

*

Loose me from Earth's Inclosure, from the Sun's
Contracted Circle set my Heart at large;
Eliminate my Spirit, give it Range   590
Through Provinces of Thought yet unexplor'd;
Teach me, by this stupendous Scaffolding,
Creation's golden Steps, to climb to Thee.

*

Something, like Magick, strikes from this blue Vault;
With just Attention is it view'd? We feel
A sudden Succour, un-implor'd, un-thought;
Nature herself does Half the Work of Man.
Seas, Rivers, Mountains, Forests, Desarts, Rocks,
The Promontory's Height, the Depth profound
Of Subterranean, excavated Grots,   910
Black-brow'd, and vaulted-high, and yawning wide
From Nature's Structure, or the Scoop of Time;
If ample of Dimension, vast of Size,
Even These an aggrandizing Impulse give;
Of solemn Thought enthusiastic Heights
E'en These infuse – But what of Vast in These?
Nothing; – (or we must own the Skies forgot):
Much less in Art. ⌐ Vain Art! Thou Pigmy-Pow'r!
How dost thou swell, and strut, with human Pride,
To shew thy Littleness! What childish Toys,   920
Thy watry Columns squirted to the Clouds?
Thy bason'd Rivers, and imprison'd Seas?
Thy Mountains molded into Forms of Men?
Thy Hundred-Gated Capitols? or Those

173

Where Three Days Travel left us much to ride
Gazing on Miracles by Mortals wrought,
Arches triumphal, Theaters immense,
Or nodding Gardens pendent in Mid-Air?
Or Temples proud to meet their Gods Half-way?
Yet These affect us in no common Kind;   930
What then the Force of such superior Scenes?
Enter a Temple, it will strike an Awe;
What Awe from This the Deity has built?

                              *

The Soul of Man was made to walk the Skies;
Delightful Outlet of her Prison Here!
There, disincumber'd from her Chains, the Ties   1020
Of Toys terrestrial, she can rove at large;
There, freely can respire, dilate, extend,
In full Proportion let loose all her Pow'rs;
And, undeluded, grasp at something Great:
Nor, as a Stranger, does she wander There;
But, wonderful Herself, thro' Wonder strays;

                              *

Of curious Arts art thou more fond? Then mark
The Mathematic Glories of the Skies: 1080
In Number, Weight, and Measure, All ordain'd;
Lorenzo's boasted Builders, Chance, and Fate,
Are left to finish his aeriel Tow'rs;
Wisdom, and Choice, their well-known Characters
Here deep-impress; and claim it for their Own:
Tho' splendid All, no Splendor void of Use;
Use rivals Beauty; Art contends with Pow'r;
No wanton Waste, amid effuse Expence;
The Great Oeconomist adjusting All
To prudent Pomp, magnificently Wise: 1090

                              *

Confusion unconfus'd! Nor less admire
This Tumult untumultuous: All on Wing,
In Motion, All! yet what profound Repose?
What fervid Action, yet no Noise! as aw'd   1120
To Silence by the Presence of their Lord;
Or hush'd, by His Command, in Love to Man,
And bid let fall soft Beams on human Rest,
Restless themselves. On yon caerulean Plain,
In Exultation to Their God, and Thine,
They dance, they sing eternal Jubilee,
Eternal Celebration of His Praise:
But, since their Song arrives not at our Ear,
Their Dance perplex'd exhibits to the Sight
Fair Hieroglyphic of His peerless Power: 1130
Mark, how, the Labyrinthian Turns they take,
The Circles intricate, and mystic Maze,
Weave the grand Cypher of Omnipotence;
To Gods, how great? how Legible to Man?

*

But Oh! – I faint! – My Spirits fail! – Nor strange;
So long on Wing, and in no middle Clime;
To which my Great Creator's Glory call'd;
And calls – but, now, in vain! Sleep's dewy Wand
Has strok'd my drooping Lids; and promises
My long Arrear of Rest: The downy God,
Wont to return with our returning Peace,
Will pay, ere-long; and bless me with Repose.   2180
Haste, haste, sweet Stranger! from the Peasant's Cot;
The Ship-boy's Hammock, or the Soldier's Straw,
Whence Sorrow never chas'd thee: With thee bring
Not hideous Visions, as of late; but Draughts
Delicious of well-tasted, cordial, Rest;
Man's rich Restorative; his balmy Bath,
That supples, lubricates, and keeps in Play
The Various Movements of this nice Machine,

Which asks such frequent Periods of Repair.
When tir'd with vain Rotations of the Day,   2190
Sleep winds us up for the succeeding Dawn;
Fresh we spin on, till Sickness clogs our Wheels,
Or Death quite breaks the Spring, and Motion ends.
When will it end with Me?

*

Thus, Darkness aiding Intellectual Light,
And Sacred Silence whispering Truths Divine,
And Truths Divine converting Pain to Peace,
My Song the Midnight Raven has outwing'd,
And shot, ambitious of unbounded Scenes,
Beyond the flaming Limits of the World,
Her gloomy Flight. But what avails the Flight
Of Fancy, when our Hearts remain below?
Virtue abounds in Flatterers, and Foes;
'Tis Pride, to praise her; Penance to perform: 2420
To more than Words, to more than Worth of Tongue,
Lorenzo! rise, at this auspicious Hour;
An Hour, when Heaven's most intimate with Man;
When, like a falling Star, the Ray Divine
Glides swift into the Bosom of the Just;
And Just are All, determin'd to reclaim;
Which sets that Title high, within thy Reach.
Awake, then: Thy Philander calls: Awake!
Thou, who shalt wake, when the Creation sleeps;
When, like a Taper, all these Suns expire;   2430
When Time, like Him of Gaza, in his Wrath,
Plucking the Pillars that support the World,
In Nature's ample Ruins lies entomb'd;
And Midnight, Universal Midnight! reigns.

176

✕ Resignation

ALL withers Here: who most possess
   Are Losers by their Gain,
Stung by full Proof, that, bad at best,
   Life's idle All is vain: 160

Vain, in its course, Life's murm'ring Stream;
   Did not its Course offend,
But Murmur cease; Life, then, would seem
   Still vainer, from its End.

How wretched! who, thro' cruel Fate,
   Have nothing to lament?
With the poor Alms this World affords,
   Deplorably content?

Had not the Greek his World mistook,
   His Wish had been most wise;   170
To be content with but One World,
   Like him, we should despise.

Of Earth's Revenue would you state
   A full Account, and fair?
We hope; and hope; and hope; then cast
   The Total up –

———
Despair
———

Notes

MARK AKENSIDE

1   Samuel Johnson, *Lives of the English Poets*, ed. G.B. Hill, 3 vols (Oxford, 1905), 3:411.
2   Laetitia Barbauld, *Essay on Akenside's Poem on the Pleasures of Imagination*, prefixed to *The Pleasures of Imagination* (London, 1795), p.v.
3   See Donald Davie, 'The Language of Science and the Language of Literature 1700-1740', reprinted in his *Older Masters* (Manchester, 1992), pp.80-117.

20 'Hymn to Science'
1   *Science* 'any art or species of knowledge' (Johnson 4). Compare the close of Blake's *The Four Zoas*: 'The dark religions are departed & sweet Science reigns' (IX, p.139:10)
6   *lab'ring mind* Locke describes 'the Workmanship of the Understanding' (in *An Essay concerning Human Understanding*, ed. P.H. Nidditch, Oxford, 1975, 3:3:12) almost exclusively in terms of arduous labour in a kind of internalised Puritan work ethic. Hence the appositeness of Akenside's stress on the pleasure (rather than the ascetic duty) of mental activity.

24 *The Pleasures of Imagination* Taken from Joseph Addison's famous series of papers on 'Taste and the Pleasures of the Imagination' in *The Spectator* (409-21, 9 June – 3 July 1712). Akenside follows these in allotting the imagination a 'middle place' between 'the organs of the bodily sense and the faculties of moral perception' (Design, p.3); in the 'three illustrious orders' of its objects, namely 'the sublime, / The wonderful, the fair' (ll.143-6); and in a variety of subsidiary interests such as synaesthesia.
1:1   *attractive* with the full Newtonian force, positing a principle of mental attraction analogous to that of gravity in the physical world.
1:17   'Combining each in endless fairy forms' (1st edn)

179

1:35-6 'The curb of rules / For creeping toil to climb the hard ascent' (1st edn)

1:39 *imp* 'to repair a hawk's wing with adscititious feathers' (Johnson 1)

1:65-6 'at large / The uncreated images of things' (1st edn)

1:109 *Memnon* the son of Tithonus and Eos, killed by Achilles at Troy, whose statue emitted sounds when struck by the first rays of the sun as a greeting to his mother, the dawn. Compare Coleridge's 'The Eolian Harp' (12-33).

1:151-221 the passage is adapted from Longinus, *On the Sublime*, xxiv (Akenside).

1:188 *vollied* 'disploded, discharged with a volley' (Johnson 1)

1:192 *redundant* 'superabundant, exuberant, superfluous' (Johnson 1)

1:194 *absolve* 'finish or complete' (Johnson 4)

1:202 *empyreal waste* Leibnitz dans la Theodicée i.19 (Akenside).

1:204 *unfading light* alluding to Huygens' hypothesis of there being stars so distant that their light had not yet reached the earth (Akenside). Compare Satan's gaze at the newly created world, *Paradise Lost* (2:1034-55).

1:297-8 the river Peneus, in Thessaly, flows through the vale of Tempe.

1:354 *pleasing call* 'awful stamp' (1st edn)

1:372-6 Compare Keats, 'Ode on a Grecian Urn': 'Beauty is truth, truth beauty, – that is all / Ye know on earth, and all ye need to know' (49-50).

1:470 *bird of Juno* swan

1:481 *Mind, mind* in the first edition even more emphatic: 'MIND, MIND alone'.

1:567 *Genius of antient Greece* compare Shelley's final chorus in *Hellas* (1060-1101).

1:592-4 the river Illusus flows through Athens; the Lyceum was the school of Aristotle; Academus the school of Plato.

2:21-3 Valclusa was the retreat of Petrarch and Laura; the river Arno flows through Florence, hence the association with

Dante and Boccaccio; Parthenope is Naples, birthplace of Tor-
quato Tasso.

2:3; *from their guardians torn* philosophy must remain 'dronish,
insipid, pedantic, useless, and directly opposite to the real
practice of the world' unless restored 'by uniting it once more
with the works of imagination; and we have had the pleasure
of observing a very great progress made towards their union in
England within these last few years. It is hardly possible to
conceive them at a greater distance from each other than at the
Revolution, when Locke stood at the head of one party, and
Dryden of the other' (Akenside).

2:39 *fane* 'temple' (Johnson 1)

2:97-120 compare Thomson's famous description of the rainbow,
Spring (186-221).

2:313 *plastic* 'having the power to give form' (Johnson 1); com-
pare 3:381.

2:579-97 compare Shelley's *Prometheus Unbound* (2:iv.43-109;
3:iv.98-204)

3:285 *inexpressive semblance* 'This similitude is the foundation of
almost all the ornaments of poetic diction' (Akenside). The
immediate issue is whether this capacity to perceive analogies
between self and world is innate or formed through early
associations (3:306-10). Roughly speaking, the 'semblance',
though 'inexpressive' because residing in 'lifeless things', is a
necessary detour by means of which 'thought and passion' can
achieve insight into themselves.

3:348 *mysterious ties* 'The act of remembering seems almost
wholly to depend on the association of ideas' (Akenside).
Compare *The Prelude* (1805) on 'those first-born affinities that
fit / Our new existence to existing things' (1:582-3).

3:351 *footsteps* 'Ideas in the Mind quickly fade, and often quite
vanish quite out of the Understanding, leaving no more
footsteps or remaining Characters of themselves, than
Shadows do flying over Fields of Corn', Locke, *Essay* 2:10:4.

3:373-90 compare the 'spirits / Of life' who 'bring the thrilling joys of sense' to Orc in Blake's *The Four Zoas*, V, and *The Prelude*, 'A plastic power / Abode with me, a forming hand, at times / Rebellious, acting in a devious mood, / A local spirit of its own, at war / With general tendency' (2:381-4).

3:401-02 *joyful sun* compare Shelley, *The Triumph of Life* (1-8)

3:478 *Mild as the breeze* compare *The Prelude*, on 'the sweet breeze of Heaven' and 'corresponding mild creative breeze' within (1:41-3)

3:604 *kindred order* compare *The Prelude* (2:440-62)

3:621 *the sun's unwearied course* compare Blake's 'The red Globule is the unwearied Sun by Los created / To measure Time and Space to mortal Men', *Milton* (29:23-4)

3:620-28 compare Coleridge's 'Frost at Midnight' (58-64), especially 'Great universal Teacher! he shall mould / Thy spirit, and by giving make it ask' (63-4).

3:633 *relish* 'delight given by anything; the power by which pleasure is given' (Johnson 5). Here elevated into a direct means of spiritual communion.

46 *An Epistle to Curio* William Pulteney (1684-1764), opposition leader and joint founder of the Patriot party in the 1730s, bought off with a title, Earl of Bath, in 1742.

Odes on Several Subjects
56 'To the Evening Star'
1-2 *Endymion* the most beautiful of men, beloved by Selene the Moon, was thrown into perpetual sleep so that every night she might embrace him.
3 *Hesper* the evening star or Venus
58 'To Caleb Hardinge M.D.'
50 *Verulamian* of or pertaining to the Earl of Verulam i.e. Francis Bacon

The Pleasures of the Imagination (revised)
4:38-45 compare *The Prelude* (1805): 'Was it for this / That one, the

fairest of all Rivers, lov'd / To blend his murmurs with my Nurse's Song . . . O Derwent' (1:272-4, 278).

4:66-70 compare *The Prelude* (1805): 'Collateral objects and appearances, / Albeit lifeless then, and doom'd to sleep / Until maturer seasons called them forth / To impregnate and elevate the mind' (1:622-5).

4:104-18 compare Blake, 'Los is by mortals nam'd Time', *Milton* (24:68-73).

JAMES MACPHERSON

1 *Boswell's Life of Johnson*, 4:183, 2:298.

2 'Annotations to *Poems* by William Wordsworth'; 'On Poetry in General', *The Complete Works of William Hazlitt*, ed. P.P. Howe, 21 vols (London, 1930-34), 5:1-18 (p.17); *William Blake: a Critical Essay* (London, 1868), p.13.

3 The Principal during this time was Thomas Blackwell, whose influential *An Inquiry into the Life and Writings of Homer* (1735) supplied two key concepts for the Ossianic poets. Firstly, that epic poetry is most successfully composed in primitive society in a period of transition and decline (hence the insistence on Ossian as the 'last of the race of Morven'); secondly, that inspiration derived from a 'Concourse of natural Causes' rather than by a 'heavenly Origin' (so pointing towards the environmental determinism of Macpherson's psychology). For further discussion see Stafford, *The Sublime Savage*, p.28 ff.

4 'On the Study of Celtic Literature', *Lectures and Essays in Criticism* in *Works*, vol. 3, ed. R.H. Super (Ann Arbor, 1962), pp.370-71.

5 *Life of Johnson*, 3:19.

6 *Prose Works*, 3:77; 1:124-5. Wordsworth's claim to authority, having been 'born and reared in a mountainous country' is, of course, equally applicable to Macpherson: see *The Hunter*, for example, on the poverty of the hill-farmer.

7   Hazlitt, *Works*, 5:18.
8   This draws heavily on the vigorous contemporary debate on the function of 'approbation', notably in Shaftesbury's *Characteristics*, Adam Smith's *Theory of Moral Sentiments*, and David Hume's *Enquiry concerning the Principles of Morals*. Put extremely baldly, the ethic of 'fame' is used to reconcile the contrasting principles of private interest and public altruism: self-love meant the pursuit of reputation which itself was achieved through acting for the common good.
9   *Life of Johnson*, 2:126.

Fragments of Ancient Poetry

81 I: 'Shilric, Vinvela'
Note how 'unperceived' stands out as the only remotely conceptual term.

82 II: 'I sit by the mossy fountain'
For a more explicitly Lockean account of the traumatic dispersal of the past, compare 'her dying image hags his fancy's eyes', *The Highlander* (3:257).

84 VI: 'Son of the noble Fingal'
In the *Fragments*, Oscian is only the most prominent among several narrators, still viewed from the outside; note how entering the story here implies a movement from outer to inner, rather than instant participation in a monologue which, for all its formalized mode of address, is almost entirely internalized.

88 *Preface to 1773 edition*   The gap between author and translator has almost completely vanished: note Macpherson's stress on 'experience', 'degree of judgement' and 'correctness' rather than imagination or original genius. Also compare Milton's preface to *Paradise Lost* on 'the troublesome and modern bondage of rhyming'.

The Poems of Ossian

89 'Cath-Loda' III

Compare Pope, 'O! while along the stream of Time thy name /
Expanded flies, and gathers all its flame', *Essay on Man* (4:383-
4), and Coleridge, 'I love to sit upon her tomb's dark grass, /
Then Memory backward rolls Time's shadowy tide; / The tales
of other days before me glide: / With eager thought I seize them
as they pass', 'Anna and Harland' (9-12).

89 'Carric-thura'

Compare Collins, 'Ode to Evening', 'while now the bright-hair'd
Sun / Sits in yon western tent' (6-7), and Blake, 'Morning': 'To
find the Western path / Right thro' the gates of Wrath' (1-2).

89 'Dar-thula'

Compare *Samson Agonistes*: 'The Sun to me is dark / And silent
as the Moon, / When she deserts the night, / Hid in her interlu-
nar cave' (86-9), and the transforming burst of moonlight in
Thomson's *Autumn* (1088-1102).

90 'Oina-Morul'

Blake uses the name Leutha for a daughter of Enitharmon in
Europe and for Satan's emanation in *Milton*.

91 'Oithona'

Gaul, engaged to Lathmon's sister and Nuath's daughter,
Oithona, is obliged to go to war with Fingal. Dunrathmon 'tak-
ing advantage of the absence of her friends, came and carried
off, by force, Oithona, who had formerly rejected his love, into
Tromathon, a desert island, where he concealed her in a cave'
(Argument). Blake reworks this triangular situation in *Visions
of the Daughters of Albion*, which also takes place in a setting of
confinement within a cave on an isolated island, and is narrated
in a similarly elliptical style, with the actual rape and abduction
only briefly alluded to, and the action primarily conducted
through an interchange of monologues. Macpherson's regular
septenary measure is also apparent beneath Blake's longer

185

line. Thematically, the major link is the transformation of Oithona, 'disconsolate and resolved not to survive the loss of her honour' (Argument) into Oothon's defiant proclamation of sexual joy. As for the other characters, Bromion perhaps has a little of Dunrommath's 'contempt'; Gaul, however, shows none of the morbid introspection of Theotormon, and is spurred to action by jealousy rather than incapacitated by it.

like a flower of the rock 'Full many a flower is born to blush unseen, / And waste its sweetness on the desert air', Gray's 'Elegy' (55-6).

95 'Carthon'

'Balclutha i.e. town of Clyde; probably the Alcluth of Bede' (Macpherson). 'The reader may compare this passage with the last three verses of the 13th chapter of Isaiah, where the prophet foretells the destruction of Babylon' (Macpherson).

'Carric-thura'.

103 *rolled into himself* Compare Blake's use of the term to denote sensual collapse: 'The Senses roll themselves in fear', 'The Mental Traveller' (63).

'Berrathon'

108 *stars . . . with their weeping eyes* compare Blake's 'The Tyger': 'When the stars threw down their spears / And water'd heaven with their tears' (17-18).

109 'The War of Caros'

carried him far away compare Wordsworth's famous lines in 'There was a Boy': 'a gentle shock of mild surprise / Has carried far into his heart the voice / Of mountain-torrents' (19-21).

109 'Carthon'

Compare Satan's address to the sun, *Paradise Lost*, 4:32-113

'The Songs of Selma'

111 *Colma* The revisions to *Fragment* X show Macpherson consciously pursuing a further simplification of an already reduced style: the unified present 'I' becomes a retrospective construct; the narrative is recollected rather than undergone; there is less dramatic address and a tendency to replace simple verbs with noun and epithet, and an insistence on the memorial context.

113 *When shall it be morn in the grave, to bid the slumberer awake?* compare Blake, 'I will arise and look forth for the morning of the grave. / I will go down to the sepulcher to see if morning breaks!', *Milton* (16:20-21)

The Six Bards

According to Macpherson, this sequence was a competition in 'extempore composition' written 'a thousand years later than Ossian'.

II:23-5 Thomas Gray commented that these lines showed 'The very Demon of Poetry', *Correspondence* eds Paget Toynbee and Leonard Whibley, 3 vols (Oxford, 1935; revised H.W. Starr, Oxford, 1971), 2:680.

122 *On the Death of Marshal Keith*

James Frances Edward Keith (1696-1758), exiled after the first Jacobite rebellion, fought as a mercenary for a variety of European powers, rose to be Frederick the Great's right-hand man, and was eventually killed fighting for the Prussians in the war of Polish succession; as a soldier, he was 'beyond question the greatest of Scots abroad' *(DNB)*.

EDWARD YOUNG

1 Revd J. Mitford, 'Life of Young', Aldine edition (London, 1853), p.xi.
2 Johnson, *Lives*, 3:394.
3 *Westminster Review* LXVII (January 1857); reprinted in *Essays of George Eliot*, ed. Thomas Pinney (London, 1968), pp.337, 366.
4 *Lives*, 3:396; Gray, *Correspondence*, Appendix Z, p.1292.
5 *Lives*, 3:398, 397.
6 Burke, *A Philosophical Enquiry into the Origin of our Ideas of the*

    Sublime and the Beaautiful, ed. J.B. Boulton (London, 1958), pp.170, 166.

7 Young, *Conjectures on Original Composition*, second edn (London, 1759), p.38.

8 The structure transposes with alarming ease onto Blake's 'corrosives, which in Hell are salutary and medicinal, melting apparent surfaces away, and revealing the infinite which was hid' within the 'bound or outward circumference' of reason (*The Marriage of Heaven and Hell*, pl.14, pl.4).

127 *The Last Day*

II:222 compare Pope's *Essay on Man*: 'And now a bubble burst, and now a world' (90)

130 *Love of Fame*

VI:210 *simplex munitiis* Horace, *Odes* 1.v.5: 'for whom this unmixed elegance'

136 *October 1745...* The 'present juncture' was, of course, the second Jacobite rebellion. Included as an example of Young's notoriously servile and overwrought epistolary style, but also to give an idea of what Macpherson's heroic warriors looked like from south of the border.

138 *The Complaint: or, Night Thoughts...*

1:8 *if Dreams infest the Grave* compare *Hamlet*, 3.i.66

1:18 *Night, sable Goddess* compare 'sable-vested Night', *Paradise Lost* (2:962), and 'the sable Throne behold / Of *Night* Primaeval', *The Dunciad* (4:629-30)

1:28-31 compare Coleridge, 'To William Wordsworth', 12-16

1:29 *antient Night* compare 'Chaos and ancient Night', *Paradise Lost* (2:970)

1:36 *Morning stars* compare Job 38:7

1:77-83 Compare *Essay on Man* (3:1-18) and note that what for Pope was a paradox beyond human reason becomes for Young further grounds for dogmatic certainty.

1:123 *vestibule* 'the porch or first entrance of a house' (Johnson 1)

1:128 *till we burst the Shell* compare Blake's Urizen, 'Build we the Mundane shell', (*The Four Zoas*, II, p.24:8)

1:155 *incrusted* compare Blake, 'an Incrustation over my Immortal / Spirit', *Milton* (40:35-6)

1:212 *Thy shaft flew thrice* Alluding to the deaths of Young's wife, Lady Elizabeth Lee, and her daughter and son-in-law in rapid succession.

1:222 *postern* Locke's term for a kind of psychic anteroom (2:3:1)

1:350 *golden mountains* compare Blake's 'golden mountains', *Jerusalem* (28:1-3)

1:357 *The Worm to riot* compare the 'invisible worm' of Blake's 'The Sick Rose'

1:371-3 *Prerogative* prior right (OED 1); *Presumption* illegal sequestering (OED 1). The recurrent technical terms are testimony to Young's legal training, and to his obsessively contractual sense of divine judgement.

1:399 from 'Man never Is, but always to be blest', Pope's *Essay on Man* (1:96)

2:35 *composition* 'the act of discharging a debt by paying part' (Johnson 9)

2:212 *horologe* 'any instrument that tells the hour' (Johnson 1)

2:273-6 *Doomsday book...leaves of Brass* compare Urizen's 'Book of eternal Brass', *The First Book of Urizen* (pl.4:32-3)

2:301-03 *Man sleeps* compare Blake's *Jerusalem*: 'Albion cold lays on his rock' (94:1)

2:356 *escutcheon'd* 'the shield of the family' (Johnson 1) often put on display after a death

2:465 *abroach* 'in a posture to run out, or yield the liquor contained; properly used of vessels' (Johnson 1)

2:487 *defecate* 'to purge liquors from leas or foulness' (Johnson 1)

3:167 *infallibility* i.e. Catholic. The original for Narcissa, Elizabeth Lee, far from receiving an unmarked grave, was respectably buried in the Swiss Cemetery at Lyons.

3:281 *pioneers* 'one whose business is to level the road, throw up works, or sink mines, in military operations' (Johnson 1)

3:324 *oughts* punning on 'orts', 'refuse, things left or thrown away' (Johnson 1)

3:342-4 *crazy* 'broken, decrepit' (Johnson 1); *concocted* 'digested by the stomach' (Johnson 1); *kennels* drains. The passage powerfully dramatizes what Blake in *There is no Natural Religion* called 'the same dull round' of the Lockean psychology. Also note Young's characteristic move from 'sense' (perception) to physical sensuality.

3:450 *'Chinks, styl'd Organs'* compare the famous lines in *The Marriage of Heaven and Hell*: 'If the doors of perception were cleansed every thing would appear to man as it is: infinite. For man has closed himself up until he sees all things thro' narrow chinks of his cavern' (pl.14), and 'Five windows light the cavern'd man', *Europe* (pl.iii:1).

3:452 *All Eye, all Ear* compare Milton's angels: 'All heart they live, all head, all ear, all eye, / All intellect, all sense' *Paradise Lost* (6:350-51)

4:96 *mighty hunter* Nimrod, Genesis 10:9

4:147 *Patriarch* Abraham

5:122 *Election* 'the power of choice' (Johnson 2); *arbitrary* 'bound by no law, following the will without restraint' in a theological sense, as well as the more familiar 'capricious' (Johnson 1 & 2)

5:958 *the sportive Goddess* Fortune

6:117 *Visto* variant of vista, 'view seen through an avenue' (Johnson 1)

6:187 *circulating Globules* compare Blake, 'For every space larger than a red Globule of Mans blood / Is visionary' *Milton* (31:19-20)

6:399-441 Cited by Wordsworth in *Tintern Abbey* in support of 'all the mighty world / Of eye, and ear, – both what they half create, / And what perceive'. M.H. Abrams, in *The Mirror and the Lamp* (New York, 1953, p.69) argues that Locke's account of perception is here transformed into its opposite, as the secondary qualities of light, taste, and colour expand into a wholly self-sufficient subjective realm. The influence of the Cambridge Platonists, particularly Ralph Cudworth, on the 'magic Organ' of imagination is frequently noted. Note, however, the initial hostility to 'the sordid Bars of Sense', and the powerful analogues of Milton's Eve, *Paradise Lost* (4:456-69) and Ovid's Narcissus, *Metamorphoses* (3:415-36).

7:126 Tiberius on Capri

7:819 *Annihilation* compare Blake's 'self annihilation' e.g. *Milton* (14:22)

7:833 *the Lumber of demolisht Worlds* compare Rochester, 'A Translation from Seneca's 'Troades', Act II Chorus'

8:245-65 Florello compare Wordsworth's 'dwarf man', *The Prelude* (5:294-349), and also Blake's absolute divide between innocence and experience.

8:522 the original 'Kouli Kan' was Nadir Shah (1688-1747), King of Persia, who conquered Moguls and occupied Delhi on one of his westward campaigns. The fantasy of absolute power has obvious relevance to Coleridge's *Kubla Khan*.

8:1106-15 compare the famous close to Blake's *A Vision of the Last Judgement*, where the 'round Disk of fire somewhat like a Guinea' seen by the 'Vegetative Eye' is transformed into 'an Innumerable company of the Heavenly host'.

9:590 *eliminate* 'thrust out of doors; expel' (OED 1)

9:1080 *Mathematic Glories of the Skies* compare 'mathematic motion wondrous' of Blake's Urizen (*The Four Zoas*, II, p.33:24)

9:2434 *Midnight, Universal Midnight!* compare 'And Universal Darkness buries All', Pope's*Dunciad* (4:627-56)